# ORELA Administrator Examination

## Teacher Certification Exam

**By:** Sharon Wynne

**XAMonline, INC.**
Boston

XAMonline, Inc.
25 First Street Suite 106
Cambridge, MA 02141
Toll Free 1-800-509-4128
Email: info@xamonline.com
Web www.xamonline.com
Fax: 1-617-583-5552

Library of Congress Cataloguing-in-Publication Data

Wynne, Sharon A.
ORELA: Administrator Examination / Sharon A. Wynne. -1st ed.

ISBN: 978-1-60787-174-3
1. Adminstrator 2. Study Guides. 3. ORELA.
4. Teachers' Certification & Licensure. 5. Careers.

**Disclaimer:**
The opinions expressed in this publication are the sole works of XAMonline and were created independently from the National Education Association, Educational Testing Service, or any State Department of Education, National Evaluation Systems or other testing affiliates.

Between the time of publication and printing, state specific standards as well as testing formats and website information may change that is not included in part or in whole within this product. Sample test questions are developed by XAMonline and reflect content similar to that on real tests; however, they are not former tests. XAMonline assembles content that aligns with state standards but makes no claims nor guarantees teacher candidates a passing score. Numerical scores are determined by testing companies such as NES or ETS and then are compared with individual state standards. A passing score varies from state to state.

**Printed in the United States of America** œ-1
ORELA: Administrator Examination
ISBN: 978-1-60787-174-3

**DOMAIN I.** Visionary Leadership and Instructional Improvement Visionary Leadership, Inclusive Practice, and Socio-Political Context

**Competency Understand strategies for facilitating the development, articulation, implementation, and stewardship of a shared vision of learning and for using inclusive practices to communicate and collaborate with families and other community members to achieve the vision and promote the success of all students**

**Skill 1.1** Demonstrating knowledge of major theories and research related to organizational and educational leadership

There are various approaches to understanding the qualities of good leaders, qualities that principals may want to emulate. The trait approach to leadership focuses on the personality traits of leaders. The situational approach postulates that leadership is a result of understanding the idiosyncrasies and characteristics of specific groups. Additionally, research from Ohio State University placed leadership in two dimensions, task and consideration. This two-factor view of leadership increased understanding of leadership behavior. Finally, another approach to understanding leadership emerged, known as the contingency approach. The contingency approach specified that the kind of leadership to be exerted depends upon a number of variables, including personality, task, group dynamics, and the situation.

Many theorists have proposed frameworks as they attempt to understand the dynamics that take place in organizations. To form its foundation, educational administration has borrowed extensively from organizational theorists.

Early organizational theorists were more concerned with how well people performed given tasks in the enterprise than with the well being of the individuals in the organization. These theories and beliefs about organizations and individuals were soon challenged by another set of theories and beliefs, which focused on the quality of relationships and the importance of people in the organization. This evolutionary pattern was followed by critical analysis of the formal and informal structures existing in organizations. The conceptualization of organizations as a system, with internal and external influences, further contributed to the base of knowledge for educational administration and leadership.

A particularly salient view of leadership within organizations was developed by Bolman and Deal (1997). Their view is that people within organizations operate within one (or more) of four organizational frames: structural, human resources, political, and symbolic. These authors argue that most leaders operate in the structural frame (focusing on hierarchies, rules, regulations, procedures, etc.) or the human resources frame (focusing on the needs of people; within schools, this could either be teachers, students, or both). The authors also argue that the two remaining frames, often ignored, are highly important for the proper running of an organization. The political frame focuses on sources of power, and the symbolic frame focuses on the symbols of organizational culture and history that are so important to employees, students, and others.

It is apparent that school administration parallels that of business organizations and other enterprises in American society. Ours is a rapidly changing world, which impacts the way organizations function. Moreover, changing situations require leaders of organizations to assess their abilities and to understand the characteristics needed to lead effectively (Lewis, 1993).

**Skill 1.2** Applying knowledge of skills, strategies, and procedures for developing, articulating, implementing, and providing stewardship of a school or district vision of learning

When principals commit to become school administrators, they have a passionate notion about how schools should work. This "vision" is often a collection of thoughts principals have developed during their teaching career or an idea that came from research or reading. The campus vision must be personalized to the campus and should include input from all stakeholders (staff, parents, community) of the individual school with the principal leading the discussion. A vision is a clear statement of the guarantee given to all students attending a certain school. Embedded in a vision is the idea of the ability to see something that is not readily apparent, or that doesn't yet exist. A school's vision should be a picture of the possibilities, reaching into a better future that will benefit the school's children.

How does one gather input about the school's vision? Every conversation with parents and other stakeholders yields information about what is important for their children. The school's history and past successes and failures are important considerations. Looking at the data found in the school's Academic Excellence Indicator System (AEIS) report will yield the facts needed to steer the stakeholders toward new areas of improvement and focus. Comparing the school's results to statewide results will also identify areas to celebrate and areas to target for improvement. The improvement targets are then delineated in the annual Campus Improvement Plan (CIP) or School Improvement Plan (SIP) document. The CIP lists the school's goals along with activities to accomplish the goals, a timeline for completion and the personnel assigned to monitor goal completion.

It has been said that everyone in a school is paying attention to what the principal is paying attention to. A principal must make sure that his/her words and actions match, and that the vision is the criteria used to identify essential needs and priorities. Principals and teachers have limited time and energy. Every task undertaken requires asking, "Will this get me and my staff closer to our vision of what we want to accomplish for children?"

**Skill 1.3** Applying knowledge of cultural competency within the educational community and its role in developing and implementing a vision of learning for all students

One of the most important jobs of an instructional leader is to change the prevailing culture of a school. Roland Barth wrote that "a school's culture has far more influence on life and learning in the schoolhouse than the president of the country, the state department of education, the superintendent, the school board, or even the principal, teachers, and parents can ever have."

Principals are charged with leaving "no child behind" and this involves a fundamental change in the culture of the school. It is no longer acceptable for the majority of students to do well. Educators are now required to ensure high levels of learning for all students. Today's school leaders must lead the staff and community in efforts to close the achievement gap between high and low performers, develop students' thinking and problem-solving skills, and attend to students' social and emotional development.

School leaders must articulate and implement an agreed vision of learning, and ensure that it is shared by the school community. Leadership to create a campus culture of high expectations requires a sense of urgency and a mix of pressure and support. If a principal is assigned to lead a school where many students are struggling, there is a need to fast track the change by pushing hard on standards, providing quality support material and examples of successful practice, and providing focused professional development. As student achievement increases, the principal should shift to capacity building to encourage local ownership. Leaders should strive to move from tighter to looser control and from external control to internal commitment.

Michael Fullan has written about the culture of "dependency" among schools—the tendency to wait for solutions from outside. Any kind of improvement is a function of learning to do the right thing in the setting where you work. Ultimately no amount of outside motivation can specify the best solutions for a particular situation. Principals who help their schools to form Professional Learning Communities (PLCs) embrace the notion that the primary purpose of a school is learning, not just teaching. Educators in PLCs examine the practices of their schools to find ways to ensure that all children will learn. Professional learning communities continuously examine what is worthwhile and how to get there.

- School staff members must work together to figure out what is needed to achieve the goal of "no child left behind".

- Internal commitment and ingenuity does not come from outside the school; expertise lies within.
- Change is forever. Problems don't stay solved, so you have to keep learning to do the right thing over and over again.

"Schools that establish high expectations for all students . . . and provide the support necessary to achieve these expectations . . . have high rates of academic success (Brook et al., 1989; Edmonds, 1986; Howard, 1990; Levin, 1988; Rutter et al., 1979; Slavin et al., 1989). Successful schools share certain characteristics: an emphasis on academics, clear expectations and regulations, high levels of student participation, and alternative resources such as library facilities, vocational work opportunities, art, music, and extracurricular activities. Conveying positive and high expectations to students occurs in several ways. One of the most obvious and powerful is through personal relationships in which teachers and other school staff communicate to students, "This work is important; I know you can do it; I won't give up on you" (Howard, 1990). Successful teachers look for children's strengths and interests, and use these as starting points for learning. A relationship that conveys high expectations to students can internalize these beliefs in students and develop self-esteem and self-efficacy.

**Skill 1.4** Applying knowledge of factors to consider in developing a vision (e.g., assessment data; learner diversity; demographics; national and state trends; research; community diversity, needs, and perceptions)

All leaders must have the capacity to plan. The ability to plan is an essential skill in today's high pressure and ever-changing school environment. It serves the very practical function of assisting administrators to organize their work and to project solutions to problems. Making a determination about what to plan for precedes the activity of planning.

Educational leaders need to plan the curriculum, to plan for students, and to plan for teachers. Planning needs emerge from problems in the environment that are identified and defined. This process must be attached to goals and objectives that are to be achieved. Who participates in the planning process is also crucial to receiving a quality and dynamic plan for implementation.

The essential foundation of planning begins with the identification of a need—a measurable discrepancy between what currently exists and a desired outcome. Through proper planning, administrators can cope with changes in the environment. Rather than acting first and thinking later, planning is a commitment to think before acting, which prevents administrators from potentially being embroiled in a set of negative consequences. Planning can be defined as a conceptualization of activities to reach an objective. Since planning and decision making often occur in the absence of all necessary information, there are inherent anticipated and unanticipated consequences. In fact, many critics argue that the current drive for "strategic planning" places too much attention on planning, which blinds school personnel from actually accomplishing their plans. On the other hand, no planning is worse than poor planning.

The process of planning yields an agreement on long term and short term goals that move the school from where it is to where stakeholders want it to be (Kaiser, 1996). Schools need to have a strategic plan that details what the school wants to accomplish over a period of time. Planning in schools is based on student enrollments, staffing projections, curriculum needs, and the vision established by stakeholders.

Administrators engage in the planning process as a means of accomplishing desired objectives and accommodating future events which can impact the school positively or negatively. Schools, being open systems, are dependent on their external environments and are subject to the uncertainties that exist in that environment. As part of planning, administrators should identify both potential support to accomplish school goals and elements that can have a negative influence on its functioning.

SKILL 1.5 Demonstrating knowledge of strategies for communicating the vision to constituents, motivating constituents to achieve the vision, and promoting community involvement in developing and implementing the vision

All parents have deeply personal reasons to support the school's efforts; they want their child to do well in school. Most parents will have strong opinions about how the principal should run a school. If they were star students, they will want the principal to replicate their school experiences. In contrast, many parents have less than positive memories of their own schooling, and these can hamper their involvement in their children's education. Principals must constantly communicate the school's vision so that parents understand what the school is trying to accomplish. Uninformed parents and community members can derail well-planned improvement efforts.

Educating parents and the community about the school's vision, programs, goals, and achievements is a key responsibility of the school principal, but such communication will be different for every school building and school community. A school's parents are as diverse as its student population, each will have varying degrees of understanding and prior knowledge. Communicating in a variety of ways will enable a school leader to reach his/her goals for parent and community involvement. Fullan writes about the power of three, that is, the power of- teachers, parents, and students working together. Involve parents and unleash a powerful force toward school improvement.

Successful principals share leadership as they reach out to their parents and community. They also work hard to expand the professional capacity of the teachers and in doing so they develop a coherent professional community. Effective leaders harness energy by creating harmony, forging consensus, setting high standards, and developing a “try this” future orientation. They are forever hopeful and lead everyone in the school’s community to share in and be driven by this hope.

------------ End of Editing Text; only formatting after this point --------------

SKILL 1.6 Demonstrating knowledge of procedures for aligning policies and practices, including accountability, to implement and achieve the vision and strategies for assessing progress in achieving the vision

To achieve the vision, the principal must work through and with others. ~~The significance of c~~Clearly defining work and outcomes is important. In this process, the principal establishes procedures to obtain feedback in a timely manner on progress toward the intended outcome(s) of work in progress. Written and oral daily or weekly progress reports serve as avenues to monitor the progress of work and to provide assistance when needed to meet established deadlines.

The progress of work should be monitored through a variety of means. Department chairpersons and grade level chairpersons are important partners in providing feedback to the principal. ~~In instances in which the~~When work is assigned across grade and curriculum levels, the chairperson of the tasks should provide~~ the~~ timely feedback to the principal. In determining how well progress is being made, the principal can use a variety of ~~techniques~~resources, such as ~~.~~ ~~N~~norm-referenced and criterion-referenced tests, observations, report reviews, checklists, team reviews, and external evaluations ~~are proven means~~ to determine how the work of others is being performed and if it is being done in a timely manner.

Principals as instructional leaders must be present on the campus, regularly visiting classrooms and providing useful feedback to teachers~~ on what is working well and what is not working well~~. Principals can provide teachers with techniques and suggestions for improving practice;~~,~~ however, principals must do so while also encouraging and showing support to teachers.

The bottom line is that we cannot, as educational leaders, hold teachers accountable at the end of the year if we do not provide them feedback within the year to let them know how they are doing.

SKILL 1.7 Applying knowledge of methods for mobilizing school, district, family, and community resources to achieve the vision, promote student learning, solve problems, and accomplish goals

The principal is the gatekeeper of a school’s resources, and resources are more than monetary. Resources include the district budget, student activity funds, Title

I and other grant monies, the human resources of parents, staff and volunteers, as well as material resources of the school building.

Every financial expenditure requires the signature and approval of the administrator. Rather than making the spending decisions based on whim or favoritism, the principal should always be guided by the campus improvement plan and the Campus Performance Objective Council (CPOC). The CPOC is also known as the campus leadership team and as required by Texas Administrative Code, the CPOC will contain members representing the school staff, the parents and the school community. For example, if funds are requested for an autism conference, but there are no school goals or student needs in this area, then this request should not be funded. However, if the school goals include literacy development, then a request for funding for additional library books may be approved.

The principal also controls the human resources, or staffing ~~of~~ the school. School staffing models vary from district to district, but all principals have some control of how many teachers and support staff are hired. Principals may make decisions about job descriptions, duties and assigned responsibilities, as well as appraisal and development of the school staff. It is a waste of human resources to have ineffective staff members continue on the school payroll, so principals should work to document and remove employees who do not contribute to the school goals. When a need for additional support surfaces, the principal must take an overall look at how staff is being used, and reallocate the human resources to meet the need. ~~An~~ For example, ~~of this happens~~ when teachers are absent and there are not enough substitute teachers to cover the classes, ~~. T~~the principal must decide ~~who will teach~~how to manage the classes~~,~~ by combining students or by reassigning office staff or support staff to fill this need.

Resources are always limited, and conflict can occur when stakeholders are denied their requests for spending. Involving the school leadership team in these decisions and keeping the group focused on student achievement will help the principal maintain integrity and will keep the focus on the school vision.

SKILL 1.8 Demonstrating knowledge of strategies for involving constituents in decision making and for collaborating with families, community members, and business, political, and service organizations to strengthen programs and support goals

**TX Skill 7.4 Use strategies for promoting collaborative decision making and problem solving, facilitating team building, and developing consensus.**

"Collaborative leadership requires a new notion of power...the more power we share, the more power we have to use." Said another way, this type of leadership is the skillful and mission driven management of important relationships. Collaborative leadership is the point at which organization and management come together. Additionally, collaborative leadership uses supportive and inclusive methods to ensure that all stakeholders affected by a decision are part of the change process.

Collaborative leaders must strive to build relationships with numerous stakeholders and create structures to support and sustain those relationships over time. There are several things that an effective school leader can do to promote collaborative decision-making and problem solving. First, it is important to identify the key stakeholders who will be helping reach the other stakeholders and decision-makers. An effective team will be built on trusting one another, embracing conflict, having accountability, making a commitment to reach goals, and staying focused.

Second, the group must develop a shared vision. This shared vision should be based on a set of core beliefs to which all stakeholders can commit. This vision also incorporates the school district's vision and goals as well as the state's standards. Paying attention and referring often to this shared vision throughout the change process is one of the most important ways for leaders to communicate effectively.

SKILL 1.9 Demonstrating knowledge of skills and strategies for creating partnerships with families, businesses, and others in the community, including using community relations models, marketing strategies, communication theory, and data-driven decision making

Planning has long been recognized as a key factor in getting the work of a school done. Mandates from superiors, desires of subordinates and others in the learning community, and a vision are but a few of the reasons that a school principal realizes the importance of planning. To develop a plan, the principal must organize all who ~~are to~~will be involved in the planning process.

In designing a plan, the school leader must ~~adhere to~~ meet~~ing~~ established deadlines, develop~~ing~~ a flow of activities, identify~~ing~~ resource allocations, and ascertain~~ing~~ evaluation strategies. The deadlines must be for today or for ~~a longer period time~~the future. Tasks to be accomplished must be prioritized with ~~with identification of~~ persons identified who ~~are to~~will accomplish each task. The principal plans for such areas as student achievement, accreditation, co-curricular activities, master schedule, parent organizations, student trips, and school special events. Managerial competencies are required to get each of these tasks accomplished.

Prior to developing a plan, the principal has to identify what needs to be done and the procedures necessary to accomplish the goals. ~~Consultation with others~~

~~in determining assigned and unassigned tasks is best accomplished through~~ E~~e~~arly involvement of ~~others who are involved or will be involved with the tasks~~participants will facilitate accomplishing tasks. The tasks may involve changing an existing situation or creating a new one to benefit the students.

To enable the school to reach its goals, planning must include the flexibility to reorder plans as unexpected activities occur. The principal must also be able to see when and from whom help is needed to achieve the goals in a timely manner. Effective communication ~~competencies are required~~allows the principal to act in proactive ways to accomplish tasks identified in plans.

Schools never have enough resources to meet all the demands placed upon them. Technology is expensive and places tremendous demands on the budget. The proactive principal understands this and makes a plan to maximize available resources. These resources include relocation, renovation, new construction, and allocation of such resources as computer quantity and location, audio-visual equipment quantity and quality, media resources and space, meeting rooms, teacher and staff offices, multi-purpose rooms, classrooms, laboratories, cafeterias, playgrounds, physical education indoor and outdoor space, and auxiliary spaces.

Some problems within a school are related to the larger community and require knowledge beyond the school. For example, if drugs are allegedly being sold a few blocks from a school and students are supposedly making purchases during the lunch hour, all information should be obtained and the community should be involved. Community involvement is critical in making a decision on how to handle this problem.

Prior to reaching a decision, the principal must gather as much information as possible from the community and the school. All potential data sources must be identified and ~~information obtained there from~~contacted. During the data gathering process, analysis of ~~the~~ information and the need~~s to explore other~~for additional sources must be explored. This process must be systematic and include such information as the source(s) of the original information, potential data sources, ways to obtain the data, means to analyze the data, who to involve and when, and how to make the decision to create the fairest and best solution(s).

## SKILL 1.10 Applying knowledge of effective media relations practices

Public information management is a systematic communication process between an educational organization and its public, both within and outside the schools. It is the exchange of two-way information, designed to encourage public interest in and understanding of, education. The principal competency *"concern for image"* in the consensus management area specifies that a principal shows concern for the school's image. This is accomplished by monitoring impressions created by students and staff. The principal manages both these impressions and public information about the school by (1) advertising successes and (2) controlling the flow of negative information.

To be effective, communication between school leaders and the public must be open, honest, and unbiased. The attitudes of parents and members of the community at large have been adversely affected by reports of the decline of American education and negative media coverage. Despite the general perception of poor public education, the majority of parents surveyed nationally expressed satisfaction with their children's schools and teachers. The most positive feedback resulted when parents felt that their concerns were being heard and addressed and that they were involved in the decision-making process.

Public relations must be carefully organized. Information deliverers must have accurate information, understand their roles in the disseminating of the information, and provide appropriate channels for feedback. The public must perceive that they are being given complete, timely information by officials who respect their feelings and sincerely want feedback. They must have an established frame of reference, i.e. know the schools' vision/mission statements, goals and objectives, and legislative issues that affect local education.

Public Relations Process

- Public information management requires analyzing the community attitude toward educational issues. The required school improvement surveys conducted each spring in many schools provide not only feedback on the issues but priorities for addressing them. Public workshops and meetings allow community members to become involved in learning about budgetary, disciplinary, and academic issues. Information gathering should be structured to obtain the most scientific results. For instance, a representative sampling is more likely from mailing surveys than from entrusting their delivery and return to students.

- The planning phase requires setting specific goals and designing the campaign to achieve these goals. During this phase, educational leaders should determine the audiences, forums, and time frames in which their message(s) will be delivered to the public. For instance, presentations to senior citizens concerning a tax increase may require a different slant than a presentation to people who have children in the schools. Issues that require voter decisions should be presented with ample time for study and cooperative decision-making or at least discussion.

- Following the communication process is equally important whether information is delivered internally or externally. Student groups are a segment of the internal public and should be treated with the same open respect as other stakeholders. The information campaign must be encoded with specific audiences in mind. Especially important is selection of the media (transmission methods) to convey the message. [Specific strategies are outlined in 2.0.] First-level media are usually in the form of newsletters to parents, press releases, and annual reports—any written document that can be distributed to the intended audiences. Follow-up transmissions include open houses, school committees or school board meetings, and educational fairs—any face-to-face communication that brings the public and school representatives together for a two-way exchange.

- Finally, school/district officials must evaluate the results of the public relations effort. Some evaluation is immediate, as in the defeat of a candidate or the passage of a bond issue. Less timely feedback can be obtained through periodic evaluations such as brief questionnaires in school newsletters, telephone surveys, or written assessments at the end of public meetings can help test the public's understanding and the level of community support.

Other Considerations

1. Schools must establish good relationships with the media. When there are more educationally-focused complaints in the "Letters to the Editor" section of the newspaper than there are news articles about school events, there is obviously a poor interaction between media and schools.

   Of course, there are several other reasons for the amount of educational coverage provided by various media.

   - Small, hometown newspapers give broader coverage to local issues/events. They may devote a whole page or section to school/classroom events.

   - Newspapers have to evaluate the "newsworthiness" of stories. Local spelling bees get better coverage than Mrs. Clarke's debate class' mock trial because one spelling bee winner in each district will compete nationally. Most newspapers consider a story of vandalism or fire at a school or a union walkout to be more newsworthy than a piece about students working at an animal shelter. Large city newspapers and television stations focus more on national and state news and regrettably often focus on educational issues that have negative or sensational.

   - Local radio and television stations may be a better venue for school news; interviews with school officials, teachers, or students; or debates on education issues that have local impact.

2. School/district publications may be more useful in providing a positive link with the community, eg: newsletters, information brochures, handbooks, and annual reports.

3. Displays of student work in public places provide visual evidence of student achievement, eg: in malls, building lobbies, and business waiting rooms.

Establishing a Good Relationship with the Media

Educational leaders must apply the communication process to public information management.

1. Ideating - Create messages that reflect understanding of the audience (the general public) and the nature of different media (newspapers, radio, television). Ask editors and producers to provide information concerning the types of material they consider newsworthy. Be available when asked to meet with reporters. Make sure press releases meet the space and time constraints of news copy.

2. Encoding - Speak in plain English avoiding educational jargon. If you must use terms such as "block scheduling" or "outcome-based education," be sure you can define, explain, or give examples that can be easily understood. Remember the receiver for whom you are encoding the message.

3. Transmitting - Be open and honest with reporters. Assume a cooperative, rather than an adversarial, posture. Be prepared to provide specific, accurate information or to direct reporters to the person(s) who can give solid answers to their questions. Refusing to answer may only lead to reporters using information from an unreliable source.

Having followed these steps, the receiver should be able to decode your message and feel free to give feedback.

SKILL 1.11 Applying knowledge of inclusive practices for interacting and communicating effectively with individuals and groups with diverse backgrounds and perspectives and for responding to diverse community interests and needs

According to Dr. James Comer, professor of child psychiatry at Yale University, ~~stated that~~ "No significant learning takes place without a significant relationship." Principals should be aware of this insight as they seek to create productive relationships in the school community regardless of the socioeconomic, ethnic or educational background of the stakeholders. Community groups, such as churches, businesses, and daycares are invaluable partners, increasing the likelihood that children will be successful in meeting the learning goals of the school.

A principal should seek out diversity on school committees so that all stakeholder groups are giving feedback about the school. When recruiting volunteers, principals should make conscious decisions to reach out to underrepresented groups. This can be done with personal phone calls, a willingness to meet at unusual times and places to accommodate work schedules, or simply asking input, even if it has to be by phone. Realizing that some people in your school community have had negative personal school-related experiences can make you more sensitive to the barriers to involvement. Principals must also realize that community members and parents are often impacted by the mental and physical fatigue stemming from economic stress. To~~When you~~ assume that the lack of involvement means a lack of caring, ~~you~~ pushes people away instead of drawing them into your school.

Here are some things that ~~you can do to~~can begin to build strong relationships with ~~the~~ diverse groups in your school community:

**Take steps to ensure that your staff knows your clientele.** Tour the community with your staff so ~~that~~ they see where the students live and what resources may be available in the community.

**Treat all visitors to your building with a high level of professionalism.** Be willing to accommodate their preferences concerning day and time for meeting, then arrive on time and be well-prepared. Schools lose credibility with parents and the community when they appear to not know what is happening with a child and/or they have no idea of what to do about it. When confronted with a problem, do not be afraid to admit mistakes. ~~If you mess up, a~~Always apologize for any mistakes.

**Administrators must ensure that all communication with the community is clear and effective.** Lack of communication and miscommunication account for nearly 80% of problems or conflicts. You can develop key communicator email lists to get word out quickly if there is a school problem, event, or need that involves the community. Utilize neighborhood newsletters and local newspapers to get the facts out about the school. Don't assume that everyone knows what you are trying to accomplish with your students. Make sure that language barriers are not an issue. Be aware of written or verbal language that is overloaded with educational verbiage.

**Make the effort to find out what the community groups are thinking and feeling.** This can be done by regularly using short surveys that address very specific topics. Make a few phone calls or visits each week to randomly ask how they think things are going at the school. Be sure to include a diverse population on your site council or school improvement team.

**Find out what the school can do to support community efforts as well.** Local restaurants may need seasonal decorations that your art classes can provide. A nursing home in the area may enjoy a holiday concert from your school choir. Local churches may need help with a variety of service projects. Older students may be able to assist with babysitting at community functions. When your school contributes to the needs of the community, you will find the community groups more willing to involve themselves in the success of the school.

**Ask the school staff to be visible in the community.** When the school staff frequents restaurants or churches, ask them to identify themselves to the people in charge. Knowing that some of the customer base comes from the local school will increase interest and participation in school events and programs by the community group.

**Don't be afraid to ask for help.** When you've invested time in building relationships with community groups, when you've actively sought their input, then you can ask for help without hesitation. Employees of local businesses may be able to come at lunch and tutor at-risk children. Donations may be given that will provide students with school supplies or other needed items. Healthcare services may be provided at low cost to families in need. Always remember to follow up with a letter of thanks for the support you receive. Involving the students in the displays of gratitude add the personal connection that will keep the community continually involved in the school.

What passes for collaboration or collegiality in many schools lacks a focus on achievement results--on short-term, formative assessment--and thus has little impact on the character and quality of teaching. When teachers engage regularly in authentic "joint work" focused on explicit, common learning goals, their collaboration pays off richly in the form of higher quality solutions to instructional problems, increased teacher confidence, and, not surprisingly, remarkable gains in achievement. Discussions about curricular issues or popular strategies can feel good but go nowhere. Principals must set aside the time for groups of teachers to meet regularly to share, refine and assess the impact of lessons and strategies to help increasing numbers of students learn at higher levels. By e~~E~~stablishing times before, after and during the school day for such collaboration, ~~is a way for~~ principals can~~to~~ eliminate isolated practice and make these planning sessions a priority. Sometimes, substitute teachers can be used to give teachers additional planning time. Principals should join these groups, not as the leader, but as a study partner, assisting in the discussion about what is working and what is not, based on student data analysis.

**Competency Understand the political, social, economic, legal, historical, demographic, and cultural contexts of education, including public school governance in Oregon and the structure of Oregon schools, and how to use this understanding to promote the success of all students**

Skill 2.1 Demonstrating an understanding of political, social, economic, legal, historical, demographic, and cultural contexts at the local, regional, state, and federal level that affect Oregon public schools and how to respond to and influence these contexts

Schools do not exist in a vacuum. T~~As such, t~~hey are characterized as open systems, signifying that they are interrelated with the environments within which they exist. The external environment of schools includes parents, businesses, taxpayers, and politicians. All of these are important to schools as their actions in one way or another affect the operations of a school. Legislatures, colleges, and other governmental or educational agencies increasingly influence schools. However, schools cannot be everything to all constituents. All organizations depend upon the environment of which they are a part for resources and other types of support. Hence, schools must maintain public relations campaigns regarding their effectiveness. As well, it is important for school leaders to know who has power and exercises power in a community.

Community aspirations and values have a significant role in the operations of a school. Schools, to an extent, serve the needs of the community where they are located. Schools must relate and react to the changing environmental conditions as they relate to the demographics of the community and the economic base. Changes in the types of jobs require an understanding on the part of the educational organization to provide education for students relevant to the demands of the local economy. Significant departure by the school from standards and norms expected in the community can cause difficulty for a school leader.

**Recently, the federal government has played a greater part in school operations. Generally, while schools once were influenced primarily by local customs and needs, they are now increasingly the subject of federally-mandated accountability systems. *No Child Left Behind*, while still leaving specific operational policies to local regulation, has put governmental and public oversight into the mix, and schools increasingly must demonstrate that they are successful in ensuring that all students meet achievement standards. Therefore, schools have been recently shaped by public perception, governmental regulation, and the fear of declining enrollment or state take-over. In many ways, this federal law has encouraged schools to become more competitive with one another for students, attention, and funding.**

SKILL 2.2 Demonstrating an understanding of the complex social, economic, and cultural factors that affect families, communities, children, and learning

Administrators must be cognizant of the complex world in which their students reside. For each individual, there is a confluence of social, economic, cultural, and financial factors that affect every component of their being. For students this is even more the case because they are often powerless to control many of the factors, yet these issues impact upon their ability to learn and to thrive. It is important that principals know and respect their students, families, and communities that they serve.

Socioeconomic differences can be among the greatest barriers to administrators being accepted in a community. It is almost automatic that a school administrator will have a personally different experience from the students and families he or she serves. Even a principal with an upbringing similar to his or her students will encounter resistance as the community views him or her as an outsider. For these reasons, it is important that the administrator is aware of the barriers that with will be erected by the community and that he or she works to remove these barriers and keep them from being built in the first place.

Savvy administrators know that it is important to gain strong allies from the very beginning. This may include courting the neighborhood clubs, little league coaches, the
"big mamas", or the elders in the neighborhood. The most connected group may change from one neighborhood to the next; however, the premise is the same. These individuals are among the most well known, most respected, and most influential figures within the community; therefore, having their supports will more likely encourage others to view the administrator with greater trust and more respect. In addition, in some communities grandparents are the caretakers and are therefore the ones who will assist the principal in reaching students and achieving the educational vision.

Wise administrators also embrace the culture of the students in a particular community. It shows respect and appreciation for the culture and allows the school leader to navigate the informal, and in some cases formal, system. Thus, in districts with a high bilingual population, it is important to learn basic phrases and cultural norms. As an example, a principal in a heavily Mexican area of East Los Angeles should learn casual Spanish, hold activities for Cinco de Mayo, and ensure that his or her school celebrates Latino heritage month. It is equally important for an administrator in Oregon to have strong cultural competence and the ability to embrace various cultures. This is because demographic patterns can change so rapidly that an administrator who is unprepared for the change will be caught unaware. During the 2000 U.S. census, it was found that 8% of all Oregonians are Hispanic. In counties such as Washington and Multnomah, this represented an increase of 245% and 170% respectively. Thus, a successful administrator must have an innate appreciation for diversity and be ready to accept and embrace students who are culturally diverse no matter what their background.

In dealing with the social contexts of students' lives, principals must be aware of changes in family situations or serious economic challenges that may be facing students. For instance, in today's difficult economic environment, many principals have had address, hunger and homelessness. At the same time, health concerns such as the H1N1 flu have added a complexity to the educational environment that challenges the most seasoned administrator. That is why it is more important than ever that an administrator internalizes the basic dispositions of being caring, concerned, and embracing of the community. In that way, he or she will be ready to face challenges head on and will increase his or her chances of providing an educational environment in which students succeed no matter the odds.

SKILL 2.3 Demonstrating knowledge of strategies for communicating and working effectively with political leaders and authorities at the local, state, and national level

The school curriculum is an action plan to educate children. The aims and goals that shape education are generated from nationwide commissions and task forces comprised of educators, and other influential citizens, including politicians. An example was the 1938 report *A Nation-At-Risk* in which the Commission on Excellent in Education reported its findings on the quality of education in America and made specific recommendations. Another example is the effort made by President Bush and state governors with the Goals 2000 effort, which emerged in 1990.

At the local level, task forces of parents, educators, and community groups impact school curriculum similar to national groups. Change is affected by data including attitudinal surveys of the students, teachers, and parent and community groups. Other data sources for curriculum selection include direct student information, such as interviews and conferences. These yield information related to dispositions for learning, likes and dislikes, as well as difficulties experienced by students due to the curriculum design or related situations. Additionally, anecdotal records held by teachers and the contents of student folders, such as testing results and report cards, may contribute to the development of profiles of students to aide in the decision-making process regarding curriculum selection. Currently, curriculum selection is a result of national concerns about reading comprehension and math and science achievement, all in the name of economic competition with other countries.

Research findings about curriculum principles and design, as well as content organization, are also valuable for decision-making. Societal expectations directly impact the objectives for learning. The *Goals 2000* movement has particularly influenced the way goals are developed. Rather than stating vague ideas, educators must now provide behavioral objectives. These types of objectives are effective because they express exactly who is to achieve what and by when, thus, success can be measured. For example, Goal Four (4) of Goals 2000 states “By the year 2000, U.S. students will be first in the world in science and mathematics achievement.” The expectations of this societal goal affected the curriculum in every state, district, and school. Even if this goal was lofty and not fully attained, it has affected the selection and content of the local curriculum.

The Commission for Goals 2000 uncovered the deplorable student achievement in math and science and by disclosing these conditions, parent, teachers, and community groups endorsed these goals as a way of improving education. Thus, the commission influenced a chain reaction where objectives were identified at the lowest levels to change the outcomes in these subject areas. As a result, subject-area goals were clearly written and became the driving force of curriculum change. The nation is also concerned with producing citizens who are prepared to transmit the ideals of a democratic society. Therefore, the school as a societal institution must include in its teaching and learning process objectives that will produce desirable learner outcomes.

SKILL 2.4 Applying knowledge of skills for understanding and responding to proposed policy changes

There are high expectations in all content areas for students in the state of Georgia. To ensure the students are successful in meeting the academic achievement goals, teachers must also be held to high standards of instruction. For most schools, this means making radical changes to their instructional practices. For administrators, attempting to change the way teachers teach and the look of their classrooms may present a real challenge. There are several reasons why teachers resist change. To compound the problem, those who have been in the profession for a while or have been at a school for a few years may be resistant to change simply if they perceive it as being the idea of a new administration. For all these reasons, principals need to be very strategic in implementing large scale changes.

An effective strategy for overcoming resistance to instructional change is to guide teachers in planning sessions. During these workshops the new, more rigorous performance standards are dissected and the staff highlights how they can implement the standards in instruction. Analysis and diagnosis of students and their data should be another focus during instructional planning. Allowing teachers to analyze test results will help them determine students' current attainment. Once instructors know where their students are currently, they can tailor lesson plans for the more challenging performance standards. As the changes are being made, success needs to be celebrated and everyone must recognize what they are doing well and honestly address shortcomings. Collaboration is still necessary but comparisons with other schools should be minimized as every school is different.

Additionally, administrators should work with teachers individually including:

- Making time to be in the classroom to help the teachers.
- Setting meetings to help teachers discuss and talk about their successes in the classroom.
- Encouraging teachers to analyze the standards so that they can easily see what the students need to learn.

One method of making sure that teachers teach the curriculum without becoming overburdened is vertical planning with colleagues, or taking a close look at the standards as they progress from one grade to another. Teachers of each grade can meet in groups to look at the standards to determine which are taught in depth in an earlier grade and which are more fully covered in later grades. This will allow the teachers to develop a list of standards that are absolutely necessary for each grade and a list of those that are stressed in another grade level.

Another strategy for helping teachers to adopt challenging performance standards is to provide professional development in planning lessons and units. If teachers plan with the end in mind, they will be able to identify what demonstrates student mastery of the specific skill taught. A third method is to use exemplars, in that way students know what demonstrates mastery.

SKILL 2.5 Using knowledge of the larger political, social, economic, legal, historical, demographic, and cultural contexts to promote positive change

Educational administration is far different from operating a business or other organization that can operate independent of the citizen's in its immediate vicinity. Educational agencies and public schools in particular, are all directly impacted by their environment. Therefore, educators must be aware of the politics, economic changes, demographic compositions, cultural contexts, and legal and historic issues that are germane to that particular environment.

Political issues will include the educational disposition of the current U.S. President and his or her administration, the policies enacted by the governor and by the state legislature, and the initiatives of local governing bodies such as the Board of Education, the mayor, and the superintendent. While all educators must be ready to implement mandates, the professional educator will also play an active role in enacting policies and procedures. By serving on professional boards, attending town hall meetings, and taking advantage of networking opportunities, a principle can do as much good for his or her school as is done when talking with students in the hallway and encouraging teachers during professional development activities. It is worth emphasizing that visibility of the administrator is ultimately to improve student outcomes. There can be no room for selfish motivations, personal gains, or other motives that compromise what could be achieved.

An administrator must also be aware of the economic and financial environments in which a school and its students reside. It is important for a school leader to have a futuristic perspective. He or she must be on the lookout for changes whether good or bad since appropriate planning can harness opportunities or mitigate damages. As an example, urban school districts are suffering greatly as factories and plants close their operations. In cities such as Detroit and Milwaukee, administrators must deal with the fallout resulting from loss of jobs, business taxes, and population numbers. Inadvertently, administrators who are able to weather the storm are the ones who saw change in the wind and who prepared to tighten belts, encourage staff members and work with all stakeholders as though the school and community were a family and every one was crucially important to surviving the maelstrom.

Demographic and cultural issues are equally important for administrators to consider. It is important to know the cultural, educational, and financial makeup of the student population, not so that preconceived notions can be reinforced or so that stereotypes can be put in place. Rather, this information will help administrators to understand potential strengths and barriers. For instance, an administrator may analyze the data and see that in the student population, 40% live in single family homes. It is likely that these students are familiar with taking on responsibilities in the home and they can be provided with leadership and volunteer opportunities at school. Likewise, this data can indicate that a coat drive may be necessary to ensure that all students are warm and comfortable when coming to school.

In addition to knowing his or her students, an administrator must also have a broad knowledge of historic and legal educational issues. This will help guide the decision making process and can ultimately save time in damage control and legal battles. The principal who understands free speech precedent will be less likely to make errors in judgment when dealing with this and similar issues.

SKILL 2.6 Knowledge of skills for communicating effectively with constituents about trends, issues, and policies affecting the school or district

In any organization or business, more than half of the administrator or supervisor's time is spent communicating with others. Good communication is essential to any educational organization; the more effective the communication process, the more successful the education process. The roles of the administrator as goal setter, task organizer, employee motivator, decision-maker, and public relations agent are facilitated by her ability to manage the communication process effectively.

Communication is the exchange of information (message) between a sender and a receiver. The process involves six steps:

1. Ideating - development of the idea or message to be communicated

2. Encoding - organization of the idea into a sequence of symbols (written or spoken words, nonverbal cues, or medium) to convey the message

3. Transmitting - delivery of the encoded message through a medium (face-to-

face, telephone, written statements, video or computer products)

4. Receiving - claiming of the message by the receiver, who must be a good reader/listener, attentive to the message's meaning

5. Decoding - the receiver's translation of the message

6. Acting - action taken by the receiver in response to the message (ignore, store, react). Feedback to the sender that the message has been received and understood is what makes communication reciprocal.

Educational leadership training programs often explain the communication process in terms of sources and channels. The main source elements are expertise, credibility, composure, and dynamism. The ability to incorporate these elements into idea presentation results in the most persuasive communication.

The means of message transmission are referred to as channels. The characteristics of channels are such elements as the need to use different media for different audiences, the need to use recognizably respected channels, the need to select mass media that serve different purposes and the recognition of personal channels as more effective than mass media in changing opinions.

**Direction of Communication (Formal)**

1. Downward - the transmission of information from people at higher levels to people at lower levels (superintendents to principals, principals to faculty and staff)

2. Upward - the transmission of information (usually feedback) from people who are at lower levels to people who are at lower levels (principals to directors of instruction, department heads/team leaders to principals)

3. Lateral (horizontal) - transmission of information between people on the same level in the organizational structure (assistant superintendent of instruction to assistant superintendent of facilities)

4. Diagonal - direct transmission of information between people at different levels in the hierarchy (usually reserved for instances when information cannot go through proper channels in a timely fashion—special reports from principals that go directly to the superintendent or assistant superintendents for transmission to the state)

A fifth form of communication exists apart from direction or formal practice—the grapevine. In actuality, the majority of information transmitted by employees laterally is carried through the grapevine. Its face-to-face informality transmits information rapidly.

Administrators should be aware of the operation of the school grapevine and incorporate its positive aspects into the communication structure. The negative aspect of unsubstantiated rumor-passing will be overridden if the administrator

- keeps employees informed about matters relevant to school or district and about issues that impact the employees' jobs

- provides employees the opportunity to express attitudes and feelings about issues

- tests employees' reactions to information before making decisions

- builds morale by repeating positive reactions/comments made by employees to higher level administrators or the community and vice versa

Teaching professionals do not like the feeling that they are being kept in the dark or are getting only partial or untimely information. Telling teachers in a faculty meeting that the district is going to reduce the faculty at their school before transfer provisions have been established will create distrust. It may seem an open gesture on the principal's part, but the timing is wrong.

**Barriers to Communication**

- The communication process requires that the sender and receiver have a common frame of reference. Because we all interpret information based on previous experience and cultural background, receivers may interpret the ideas in messages differently than the sender intended. For example, information, delivered during contract negotiations, is interpreted differently by union representatives than by district contract negotiators. These distorted perceptions arise because the participants are operating from different frames of reference. To make the communication effective, all parties must realize the specific goal of the talks is to spend funds in the most educationally sound manner, not to deprive either group of its just desserts.

- Filtering is a barrier that occurs during transmission of information from one level to another. It may be intentional or unintentional. In downward communication, it may be the omission of some of the message or improper encoding for the intended audience. Administrators frequently deliver information only on a need-to-know basis or deliver only positive information, fearing that negative information will damage the decoding process. This succeeds only in causing the receivers to be confused as to the message's intent or to feel patronized. In upward communication, employees may limit information to those facts that shed favorable light on their personal performance because of previous experience with inconsistent or arbitrary evaluations.

- Another barrier results from improper listening skills. The receiver must heed the entire message, decode it non-judgmentally, and seek clarification of any unclear points. This happens best when the sender creates a non-threatening environment in which the listener can practice non-evaluative listening.

- Biases against race, gender, or status can prejudice receivers against a message. Senders can suggest bias by words, nonverbal clues, and attitudes. A male principal with chauvinist attitudes may alienate female teachers; a male teacher who resents a female principal may tune her out.

Overcoming these barriers becomes an administrative responsibility. To establish effective communication, the supervisor should

- establish trust by sincerely correlating her message and behavior. Never being available after stating the existence of an open-door policy will ~~not create~~undermine trust.

- listen carefully and provide open channels for feedback. Avoid giving non-verbal cues that contradict the message.

- understand and respect employees' needs, interests, and attitudes. Allow discussion, even disagreement. The important thing is that employees know they are being heard.

- time information delivery properly. Timing affects the manner in which employees perceive the message. Avoid leaking partial information. Transmit accurate information in time for employees to provide feedback.

- use appropriate media for transmitting the message. Written or face-to-face communication is necessary when the message ~~is of~~ concerns ~~to~~ a single receiver or when the message ~~is of immediate~~ concerns ~~to~~ a group with common interests. Oral or video presentations are appropriate for delivering~~y of~~ information that affects a department or faculty, such as safety measures or reporting abuse.

The educational leader must be adept in the many skills of communication.

## SKILL 2.7 Demonstrating knowledge of how to mobilize community support and actively advocate for policies, laws, programs, and instructional strategies that promote equity and success for all students

To ensure equity and access for all students, the administrator must first internalize that this is a noteworthy and important goal. A school leader should have a commitment to implementing policies and procedures that lead to success of all students. When this goal drives the educational efforts, it will be easier for the administrator to mobilize support for the community. Researchers have identified several steps necessary to gain community supports. These steps are transferable whether the leaders are trying to launch a healthcare effort, prevent criminal activity in the neighborhood, or diffuse an educational program that is beneficial to students.

In the first stages of community mobilization, it is important to recognize formal and informal networks that exist. Formal networks include organizations such as neighborhood watches, churches, political action groups, and social networks. Informal networks include any connections of people where information is shared, decisions are made, and actions are supported. Often, leaders overlook informal networks, which can be more effective than the formal ones. Upon identifying the networks, step two is to solicit and gain buy-in. This can be accomplished through town hall meetings or other forums that allow the democratic process to operate. The University of Florida (2002) has provided a manual that outlines several steps for successful community mobilization. While the entire document can be accessed on their website, http://wch.uhs.wisc.edu/docs/PDF-Pubs/MobilizingTheCommunity-9.pdf , the steps can be summarized as follows:

1. Identifying the need and rallying community members to devote time to addressing the need
2. Holding town hall meetings or events that allow for open, organized dialogue
3. Providing sign-up sheets and subcommittee options for activists to work together
4. Facilitating the work of the subcommittee, volunteers, and grassroots word-of-mouth advocates
5. Engaging in a systematic, ongoing public relations efforts to diffuse the message throughout the community to all stakeholders
6. Anticipating problems and roadblocks and implementing strategies to mitigate their impact
7. Celebrating the success of the efforts, and highlighting all participants and stakeholder groups who assisted in the process

Following these steps will provide greater stability to the efforts and ensure greater success for any educational initiative. Social sciences suggest that leaders be highly cognizance of the politics and challenges of community mobilization. It is unwise to approach this process was less seriousness than one would take when lobbying legislators or working in formal political networks. Therefore, it is advisable for administrators to establish and nurture strong community ties very early in their tenure. It is through trust building, and ongoing relationships that effective mobilization efforts can be launched around any issue no matter how challenging. Likewise, a soft or unreliable network will make it difficult for an administrator to achieve even the most laudable educational goals.

## SKILL 2.8 Demonstrating knowledge of public school governance in Oregon, including relevant laws and regulations

a. types and structure of school districts,
b. procedures for the election of school boards,
c. roles and responsibilities of school boards and superintendents,
d. the influence of the Oregon legislative system,
e. ways to interact with this system to advocate for children, schools, and school districts

Information on the governance of Orgeon's educational system can be obtained on the website: http://www.ode.state.or.us/search/page/?=2011. This section of the Xamonline study guide will contain either summaries or direct excerpts from the site. The content will not be exhaustive; therefore, it is important that each reader access the state website and become familiar with the information it contains.

The State Board of Education, with seven members appointed to four-year terms by the governor, is charged with establishing policy for the administration and operation of the public elementary and secondary schools and public community colleges in the state. Oregon's current Superintendent of Public Instruction, Susan Castillo, has served since being elected in May 2002, and sworn in on January 6, 2003. The Superintendent established six priorities for the Oregon Department of Education:

1. Ready For School - Full-Day Kindergarten For Title I Schools
2. Success For All Students - Closing The Achievement Gap
3. Learning To Read/Reading To Learn - Literacy At Every Grade
4. School and District Leadership
5. Every School A Community School
6. Learning For Success - Improving Middle And High Schools

The State of Oregon's public education system consists of public school districts and education service districts with their own respective governing bodies. The Oregon Legislature created the Oregon State Board of Education to set the educational policies and standards of Oregon's state schools and community colleges. Its mission is to "consider the goals of modern education, the requirements of a sound, comprehensive curriculum best suited to the needs of the students and the public and any other factors consistent with the maintenance of a modern and efficient elementary and secondary school system and community college program" (ORS 326.011).

The Oregon State Constitution of 1859 established a system of common schools, and designated the governor as Superintendent of Public Instruction with the provision that after five years the Legislative Assembly would be allowed to create an independent office for this purpose (Const., art. 8). The Legislative Assembly exercised this right in 1872 by enacting a law designating an elected four-year position, salary, and providing office space in the state capital (O.L. 1872, p. 146).

GENERAL PROVISIONS

**334.003 Definitions.** For purposes of this chapter:

(1) "Component school district" means a common school district or a union high school district located within the territory of an education service district.

(2) "Education service district" means a district created under ORS 334.010 that provides regional educational services to component school districts.

(3) "Joint school district" means a common school district or a union high school district located within the territory of more than one education service district. [1995 c.611 §20; 2001 c.518 §1]

**334.005 Mission; purpose; accountability.** (1) The mission of education service districts is to assist school districts and the Department of Education in achieving Oregon's educational goals by providing equitable, high quality, cost-effective and locally responsive educational services at a regional level.

(2) An education service district plays a key role in:

(a) Ensuring an equitable and excellent education for all children in the state;

(b) Implementing the Oregon Educational Act for the 21st Century;

(c) Fostering the attainment of high standards of performance by all students in Oregon's public schools; and

(d) Facilitating interorganizational coordination and cooperation among educational, social service, health care and employment training agencies.

(3) An education service district's role is one of leadership and service. Education service districts shall maintain the distinction between their role as service organizations and the regulatory role of the Department of Education and other state agencies.

(4) To ensure that an education service district is locally responsive, an education service district shall provide:

(a) Opportunities for component school districts to participate in decisions about the services that are offered by the education service district; and

(b) A variety of flexible service delivery models.

(5) An education service district shall remain accountable to:

(a) The public at large;

(b) The component school districts; and

(c) The State Board of Education. [1963 c.544 §1; 1975 c.477 §1; 1983 c.610 §2; 1993 c.784 §1; 2001 c.518 §2]

**334.010 Education service districts.** There is created in each region a district to be known as the education service district to consist of the counties and the area of the common school districts as listed in ORS 334.020, with a governing body thereof to be known as the education service district board. [Amended by 1961 c.153 §1; subsections (3) and (4) enacted as 1961 c.153 §2; 1963 c.544 §29; 1965 c.100 §170; 1977 c.481 §1; 1993 c.784 §2]

**334.020 Composition of education service districts.** (1) On and after the effective date of the order entered under section 25, chapter 784, Oregon Laws 1993, except as the boundaries of an education service district may be changed by merger under ORS 334.710 to 334.770 or other provision of law, the education service districts are as follows: (21 districts are then listed)

(2) Where a boundary change or formation of a component school district results in a joint school district, the joint school district shall be included in the education service district in which the joint district's administrative office is located. [Amended by 1957 c.678 §2; 1963 c.544 §30; 1965 c.100 §171; 1975

c.770 §39; 1993 c.784 §3; 1995 c.611 §6]

**334.022 No distinction in state funding between multicounty and single county districts.** In adopting any rule relating to the distribution of state funds to education service districts, the State Board of Education shall not make any distinction based on the administrative structure of multicounty education service districts and the administrative structure of single county education service districts. [1993 c.784 §38]

**Note:** 334.022 was enacted into law by the Legislative Assembly but was not added to or made a part of ORS chapter 334 or any series therein by legislative action. See Preface to Oregon Revised Statutes for further explanation.

EDUCATION SERVICE DISTRICT BOARD

**334.025 Number of board members; election; local advisory committees.** (1) The board of directors of an education service district shall consist of seven, nine or 11 members.

(2) In education service districts, not fewer than five of the directors shall be elected, one from each of the zones established under ORS 334.032. At the discretion of the board of directors, one or two board members may be elected from the district at large.

SUPERINTENDENT

**334.225 Superintendent; duties; compensation.** (1) The education service district board shall employ a superintendent who must hold an administrative license as a superintendent. The superintendent shall serve as the board's executive officer, give an official bond or an irrevocable letter of credit issued by an insured institution, as defined in ORS 706.008, and have the duties prescribed by the board and the laws of this state. The board shall fix the term and compensation of the superintendent, provide office room for the superintendent and allow all of the superintendent's necessary traveling expenses.

(2) The education service district board shall designate the superintendent as the district clerk. The board may appoint qualified persons as deputies to the superintendent to perform the duties required of the district clerk by law or by the board. [Formerly 334.120; 1975 c.278 §9; 1975 c.477 §9a; 1983 c.379 §9; 1985 c.195 §1; 1991 c.331 §56; 1997 c.631 §462]

**Competency Understand methods for designing and implementing an effective, research based instructional program and for promoting a positive school culture that emphasizes student learning and achievement**

Skill 3.1 Demonstrating knowledge of the characteristics, strengths, and limitations of various instructional research methods

**Scientifically Based Research (SBR)**

The No Child Left Behind (NCLB) Act requires educational programs and practices to be grounded in scientifically based research. Scientifically based research (SBR) is defined in the NCLB legislation as "research that involves the application of rigorous, systematic, and objective procedures to obtain reliable and valid knowledge relevant to education activities and programs" (NCLB, 2002). The imperative for incorporating SBR is dictated not only by federal law, but by common sense as well. With budgets tighter and district demands greater, educators need to be able to evaluate the evidence for the effectiveness of costly programs and materials. SBR is the "gold standard" for such evidence (Coalition for Evidence-Based Policy, 2003).

**NCLB Programs That Require SBR**

- Title I directs funds toward improving the academic achievement of the disadvantaged. Title I funds are directed toward improving basic programs operated by school districts, Reading First and Early Reading First, Comprehensive School Reform, Even Start, and improving school libraries. All of these funds must be directed toward programs and materials that are grounded in SBR.

- Title II directs money toward preparing, training, and recruiting high-quality teachers and principals. It also provides grants for math and science partnerships. These funds may support only those interventions that show evidence of effectiveness in improving student performance.

- Title III addresses language instruction for limited-English-proficient and immigrant students. It mandates that all curricula for teaching these students be tied to SBR criteria.

- Title IV, also known as 21st Century Schools, funds programs that promote safe and drug-free schools and communities, as well as 21st Century Community Learning Centers. Both kinds of programs need SBR supporting their effectiveness.

The U.S. Department of Education (Comprehensive School Reform Program Office, 2002) has identified the following questions to ask when judging the quality of implementation and replicability.

- How many schools have used this practice or program?
- Did the schools using it fully implement the practice or program?
- In what settings has it been implemented?
- Has improved student achievement been convincingly demonstrated in a variety of settings?

The U.S. Department of Education (Coalition for Evidence-Based Policy, 2003) has provided guidelines for a school to judge whether the research base of an educational intervention provides evidence of effectiveness:

- Strong evidence of effectiveness requires experimental studies of high quality (i.e., studies that meet all the criteria detailed in the previous section). Moreover, the research must demonstrate effectiveness in at least two typical school settings (i.e., using regular schools and classroom teachers), including a setting similar to the school considering whether to implement the program.
- Possible evidence of effectiveness requires quasi-experimental studies of high quality (i.e., studies that carefully match the treatment and control groups and that meet the criteria discussed in the previous section), or experimental studies that do not meet all the criteria for quality.

Gathering, synthesizing, and using SBR are the steps to making good decisions about educational programs, products, and practices. Although studying the evidence base is time consuming, proper consideration of SBR gives educators greater confidence in their decision making and may lead to greater opportunity for students to succeed.

- Decision makers should understand the importance of research. Just as leaders in business and industry use research to improve their products and services, so too school leaders should utilize research to inform their decisions about school programs.
- Administrators and teachers should have a grasp on the fundamental principles of research. This will allow them to understand the strengths and limitations of the research behind a given school program or product. It is true that school leaders have neither the time nor training to offer expert critiques of educational research. Nevertheless, if they understand basic concepts of research—such as comparison groups, measurement quality, and replication—they will have the basic vocabulary to comprehend the critiques of those who are qualified to offer them. This will help school leaders make more informed decisions about how to select the right programs and products for their schools.

**Pitfalls of SBR**

Perhaps the greatest pitfall to the use of SBR is the small number of experimental studies about important topics in education. Due to the federal requirements regarding SBR, many vendors are touting their products and services as "evidence based."

There is likely to be confusion between programs that are based on scientific research and programs which themselves have been rigorously tested (Slavin, 2003). This distinction is subtle yet important: The individual components of a program may all be supported by research, but the way that the program organizes and emphasizes the components may not be supported by research. The experience of the New York City schools in selecting a reading curriculum is a case in point. School officials selected a reading program whose major components were amply supported by research. Yet, in the view of some critics, the program *itself* had not been rigorously tested and, therefore, was not sufficiently scientifically based. As a result, the New York City school district had to switch its reading program in order to ensure federal funding (Manzo, 2004).

Another pitfall is overreliance on SBR. Potentially, a school can be so swayed by the evidence for the effectiveness of an educational program that it might fail to verify whether such a program is a good match for its own conditions and needs. Administrators must look beyond the evidence for a program's effectiveness and also consider evidence for successful implementation in schools similar to theirs.

Finally, the limited amount of time for educators to study the research can be a pitfall. Reviewing the research literature is a time-consuming process. One resource for identifying evidence-based practices is the What Works Clearinghouse (WWC), sponsored by the U.S. Department of Education.

**Scientifically Based Research on Reading**

Good reading programs

- use valid screening measures to find children who are at risk and provide them with effective, early instruction in phonology and oral language; in word recognition and reading fluency; and in comprehension and writing skills;
- interweave several components of language (such as speech sounds, word structure, word meaning, and sentence structure) into the same lessons;
- build fluency in both underlying reading skills and text reading, using direct methods such as repeated readings of the same text;
- incorporate phonemic awareness into all reading instruction, rather than treating it as an isolated element;
- go beyond the notion of phonics as the simple relationship between letters and sounds to include lessons on word structure and origins;
- build vocabulary from the earliest levels by exposing students to a broad, rich curriculum; and
- support reading comprehension by focusing on a deep understanding of topic and theme rather than just a set of strategies and gimmicks.

Skill 3.2 Applying knowledge of how to use research and various types of data to develop, implement, and assess instructional programs and improvement plans aimed at enhancing student achievement

When making decisions or solving problems, administrators should gather data from a number of sources, including classroom observations, interviews and discussions with students, discussion with teachers and parents, testing and measurement data, information from pupil services or guidance services, and surveys of the school and school community.

This systematic process may require information ranging from grade level surveys of needs to school-wide surveys. This practice will not have full impact unless careful attention is given to a cohesive set of goals developed jointly with administrators, teachers, parents, and members of the school community to address specific needs. It is important that the instrument gathers pertinent information related to students' needs and the program environment at the school. Once the instrument is administered and the results are quantified, analyzed, and interpreted, the direction to follow is then determined.

For program development, goal statements are carefully stated and established, and goals are prioritized and linked to performance outcomes of the students. A needs assessment can be used and it typically follows a sequence where data is collected, organized, and reported to stakeholders. High-priority goals are implemented with specific strategies delineated. However, if the purpose of the assessment is to progress check, then the assessment instrument should reflect statements concerning activities and functions of the students and the staff, as well as communication between the various levels. The systematic assessment of school needs should go beyond surveys to include cumulative folder content, anecdotal records, test results, interviews, classroom sociograms, direct teacher observations, and other means deemed appropriate.

Skill 3.3 Applying knowledge of how to use assessment and data analysis to report on progress and ensure educational accountability

Educational accountability has taken on a whole new meaning for administrators and teachers in the past decade. Large scale assessment of students at the end of the school year can make or break a school. Schools that do not perform well on these assessments are often subjected to sanctions or decreased funding and even the firing of teachers and administrators. Test results are published so that schools and school districts are compared with one another and where school choice is permitted, parents often decide to place their children in schools with high scores on the tests.

For administrators, this presents a challenge. Every classroom is different and high scores one year do not necessarily translate into high test scores in the following year. The first step is to analyze the scores and determine where there are successes to celebrate and where more work needs to be done. It is imperative that there be internal accountability so that all teachers take responsibility for the students' learning. The social studies teacher, for example, can work with the English teacher, so that the same objectives are covered in both classes.

The administrator should not only analyze the test scores to see where changes can be made, but test results should also be analyzed in order to determine the school's potential. Then, through consultation with the teachers, a plan can be devised to help bring about school growth and improvement. By comparing the practices of high achieving schools with those of your school, you can bring about gradual change that will improve the instruction in your building. Best practices will become part of the school setting as teachers meet to discuss problems and areas where they have experienced success.

By using best practices, schools can recognize areas of concern and take steps to effect change. This may mean adjusting practices in the classroom so that they meet the needs of all students. Ongoing assessment is a necessity to help teachers determine what students know and what they still need to learn. Through using the data from classroom assessments, teachers are better equipped to help students succeed.

## Scores on the FCAT

The Florida Comprehensive Assessment Test (FCAT) is the primary measure of students' achievement of the Sunshine State Standards. Student scores are translated into a school grading scale in order to ascertain how well a school is functioning. Score are classified into five achievement levels, with 1 being the lowest and 5 being the highest. Schools earn one point for each percent of students who score in achievement levels 3, 4, or 5 in **reading**, one point for each percent of students who score 3, 4, or 5 in **mathematics,** and one point for each percent of students who score 3, 4, or 5 in **science**.

## SCHOOL GRADING SCALE

**A**

525 points or more
Meet adequate progress of lowest students in reading and mathematics
Test at least 95% of eligible students

**B**

495-524 points
Meet adequate progress of lowest students in reading and mathematics within two years
Test at least 90% of eligible students

**C**

435-494 points
Meet adequate progress of lowest students in reading and mathematics within two years
Test at least 90% of eligible students

**D**

395-434 points
Test at least 90% of eligible students

**F**

Fewer than 395 points OR
Less than 90% of eligible students tested

## Making Annual Learning Gains

Since FCAT **reading and mathematics** exams are given in grades 3 – 10, it is possible to monitor how much students learn from one year to the next. Students can demonstrate learning gains in any one of three ways: *Improve* achievement levels from 1-2, 2-3, 3-4, or 4-5; **or** *Maintain* within the relatively high levels of 3, 4, or 5; **or** *Demonstrate more than one year's growth* within achievement levels 1 or 2 (does not include retained students).

Special attention is given to the reading and mathematics gains of students in **the lowest 25%** in levels 1, 2, or 3 in each school. Schools earn one point for each percent of the lowest performing students who make learning gains from the previous year in reading and mathematics. It takes at least *50%* in both reading and mathematics to make "adequate progress" for this group. Schools that fall short of 50% can still meet the requirement if they show annual improvement in this percentage.

Schools that do not make adequate progress with their lowest students in reading and mathematics must develop a School Improvement Plan that addresses this need. If a school, otherwise graded "A", does not demonstrate adequate progress in the current year, the final grade will be reduced by one letter grade. If a school, otherwise graded "B" or "C", does not demonstrate adequate progress in either the current or prior year, the final grade will be reduced by one letter grade.
For more information on Florida's School Grading System see:
http://schoolgrades.fldoe.org/pdf/0708/SGGuide2008.pdf

Skill 3.4 Demonstrating knowledge of how to use technology and information systems to enrich curriculum and instruction, monitor instructional effectiveness, and assist educators in promoting positive change

One of the major impediments to establishing successful computer-based applications in schools is the lack of careful and extensive planning (Picciano, 1998). Kearsley (1995) wrote that the role of leadership in schools requires the ability to identify how computers can improve the efficiency of school operations. He ~~continues, stating that~~also suggests a school leader must adjudicate computer use so that it serves the interests and needs of all school constituents. A specific list of competencies is associated with school leaders' ability to make policy and decisions governing the use of technological resources. A school leader must have knowledge of computer terminology and its~~, a knowledge of~~ instructional and administrative applications, and an understanding of the impact of technology in the school environment.

An essential ingredient of good administration is planning. A school leader must plan for all aspects of integrating technology in a school. The determination of hardware and software are essential~~s~~ in the process. The identification of goals and objectives for the introduction of technology is also important. Missing components from a computer system that is expected to be implemented nullifies~~thwarts~~ the ~~ability~~ effective use of technology~~ to be used to its potential~~. To ensure that computer implementation proceeds unhindered from problems, ~~it is important to have~~ policy statements and procedures governing technology must be in place.

The introduction of technology in a learning environment should not be based on technology for technology's sake, but rather on a calculated and planned agenda to which technology will be used to address identified needs. Will the introduction of technology address productivity, administrative functions, or will its introduction address student achievement? In each of the situations, a different set of resources, policies, and decisions regarding the implementation will need to occur. An administrator's depth of understanding regarding salient issues in each area is required to make informed decisions.

The classroom environment, in many instances, is characterized by teachers being at the center of attention, performing, and students acting as passive vessels, consuming knowledge and information. A learning environment characterized by technology, however, offers a much different scene, and~~, of course, a very different mode of instruction and interaction. When technology is a part of the learning process,~~ a different model of teaching and learning unfolds. It is a student-centered, constructivist model, where students are challenged to engage in higher order thinking skills, interact with technology at their own level, and learn what interests them.

Jonassen (1996) discusses how computers in the classroom become powerful tools for learning when they are applied in the learning process. Specific applications, like databases and spreadsheets, become key elements of the learning process, allowing students to integrate and relate content ideas (Jonassen, 1996).

Skill 3.5 Demonstrating knowledge of factors to consider in developing an instructional program (e.g., student characteristics and needs, state content and English Language Proficiency standards, requirements of No Child Left Behind [NCLB]) and methods for allocating resources to sustain the instructional program

The No Child Left Behind Act addresses accountability of school personnel for student achievement with the expectation that every child will demonstrate proficiency in reading, math, and science. For example, all students should know how to read by grade three. The general education curriculum should reflect state learning standards.

At the same time, flexibility and creativity may be required to help a student achieve. For example, teachers in grades K-3 are mandated to teach reading to all students using scientifically based methods with measurable outcomes. Some students (including some with disabilities) will not learn to read successfully unless taught with a phonics approach. Therefore, incorporating phonics into the reading program may be necessary.

Another example: Students are expected to learn mathematics. While some students will quickly grasp the mathematical concept of groupings of tens (and further skills of adding and subtracting large numbers), others will need additional practice. Research shows that many students with disabilities need a hands-on approach. Perhaps those students will need additional instruction and practice using snap-together cubes to grasp the grouping-by tens concept.
This means that students with special needs, such as those with a physical or mental disability or an emotional problem, generally require specific educational planning. Based on the unique needs of the child, such programs are documented in the child's Individualized Education Program (IEP), as dictated by the Individuals with Disabilities Education Act (IDEA).

In Florida, parents of students with disabilities can utilize the McKay Scholarships for Students with Disabilities Program. According to the provisions of s. 1002.39, it allows parents who are dissatisfied with their student's progress to request and receive a McKay Scholarship to then attend a private school. Such provisions typically exist because special education services at the district level may be ineffective or even negligent.

In the best case scenario, the school district and the principal ensure that all students who need special services receive them. Favorable outcomes result when there is effective collaboration between general and special education teachers, and the school works to develop a truly individualized plan. A team consisting of appropriate personnel – such as the special education coordinator, school psychologist, social worker, guidance counselor and/or nurse – along with the principal as needed, should work together with classroom teachers to develop a plan of action for each student. The team also needs to work collaboratively with parents, students, and community personnel in the development of clear, measurable goals and objectives that are aligned with district, state and federal standards.

**Creating Effective Individualized Education Plans**

Assessment results usually provide basic information contributing to the development of a good Individualized Education Plan (IEP). These results need to be clearly interpreted. When first looking at assessment results, it is most beneficial to identify skill areas closest to grade level expectations. Since the student is demonstrating some skills very close to grade level, the team needs to think of what simple adaptations can be made to the regular curriculum to allow the student to achieve success. There are numerous adaptations and modifications available from many different sources that could be implemented easily to provide success, from providing outline of the information to allowing extra time to complete written assignments.

Once all of the possible adaptations have been made then it is time to look further. Skills that are significantly below grade level require more than simple

adaptations. The team needs to consider what strategy can be implemented that will help the student make up the lost ground. It is not enough for the student to simply progress; the goal is to catch the student up to grade level in the shortest amount of time possible and to achieve to the best of his or her ability.
After the plan has been made, it is imperative that the team continually monitor the progress the student is making. Using regular weekly or bi-weekly monitoring, the team can make timely adjustments to the student's educational plan. Further, regular assessment can also be valuable in ensuing that an IEP is adequate.

Students in grades 3 through 11 take the FCAT exams. These tests indicate how much the students have learned and help to indicate how well the school's instructional program is functioning. Other forms of assessment may also be needed, utilizing both school and community resources.

Students with disabilities (in all areas) may demonstrate difficulty in academic skills. A student with mental retardation will need special instruction across all areas of academics while a student with a learning disability may need assistance in only one or two subject areas. Students with disabilities may demonstrate difficulty with independence or self-help skills. A student with a visual impairment may need specific mobility training while a student with a specific learning disability may need a checklist to help in managing materials and assignments.

Teachers and administrators should be aware that although students with disabilities may demonstrate difficulty in similar ways, the causes may be very different. For example, some disabilities are due to specific sensory impairments (hearing or vision), some due to cognitive ability (mental retardation), and some due to neurological impairment (autism or some learning disabilities). The root causes of behavioral or emotional problems may be multi-faceted, including genetic disposition, traumatic stress, biochemical imbalances, current family issues and other factors. The reason for the difficulty should be a consideration when planning the program of special education intervention.

Additionally, educators should be aware that each area of disability has a range of involvement. Some students may have minimal disability and require no services. Others may need only a few accommodations and have 504 Plans. Some may need an IEP that outlines a specific special education program which might be implemented in an inclusion/resource program, self-contained program, or in a residential setting. A student with attention deficit disorder (ADD) may be able to participate in the regular education program with a 504 Plan that outlines a checklist system to keep the student organized and additional communication between school and home. Other students with ADD may need instruction in a smaller group with fewer distractions and would be better served in a resource room.

For more information about assisting students with disabilities related to learning and the Florida Sunshine State Standards, including the Standards for Special Diploma, go to http://www.cpt.fsu.edu/ese/.

Skill 3.6 Applying knowledge of strategies for developing and maintaining a positive culture of learning that capitalizes on and is responsive to student diversity

Educational leaders have a duty and responsibility to become attuned to the specific needs and issues relevant to all socio-cultural groups represented in their school district and community. Without such attunement, administrators are not able to adequately provide leadership and services to some students and families. In order to be effective across many cultural groups, school leaders must develop cultural competence and cross-cultural communication skills.

Developing cultural competence does not happen overnight or simply by attending a training workshop on the topic. It is an ongoing process of self-reflection, learning and skill development. Developing an understanding of one's own values, attitudes and awareness of diversity is a first step. Moving beyond cultural sensitivity to cultural competence in a school setting involves learning about other cultural beliefs and attitudes, particularly in relation to schools and institutions, and then developing skills that enable the counselor to relate and communicate well with people of differing socio-cultural backgrounds.

One area that is important to understand is the significance of cross-cultural interactions: how different groups have historically interacted with each other, especially within the context of institutions such as schools and health care systems. Many minority groups, especially people of color, have been mistreated by and underrepresented in many societal institutions. These negative experiences and the resulting distrust can make cross-cultural communication challenging for school counselors at times.

Acquiring cross-cultural skills aimed at respect, trust-building, and effective communication is essential in achieving cultural competence. Further, institutional policies and practices need to be changed as well. Minority groups need to be represented at all levels of the school administration and staff to reach cultural competence, and school practices need to better accommodate and respond to the cultural needs of all students and families.

Two websites that offer more detailed information about cultural competence are cecp.air.org/cultural/default.htm and www11.georgetown.edu/research/gucchd/nccc/foundations/frameworks.html.

**Federal Laws Prohibiting Discrimination**

*Title VI, The Civil Rights Act of 1964* extends protection against discrimination on the basis of race, color, or national origins in any program or activity receiving federal financial assistance. *Clark v. Huntsville, Tyler v. Hot Springs*

*Title VII, The Civil Rights Act of* 1964 states that it is unlawful for an employer to discriminate against any individual with respect to compensation, terms, conditions, or privileges of employment because of an individual's race, color, religion, sex, or national origin. Some exceptions are noted in this statute. It does not apply to religious organizations that seek individuals of a particular religion to perform the work of that organization. Where suspect classifications (those classifications having no basis in rationality) represent bona fide occupational qualifications, they are permitted. Classifications based upon merit and seniority are also acceptable under this statute. *Ansonia BOE v. Philbrook*

*Title IX, The Educational Amendments of 1972* states that no individual shall be excluded from participation in, be denied the benefits of, or be subjected to discrimination under any educational program or activity that receives or benefits from federal assistance on the basis of sex. This statute covers the areas of admission, education programs and activities, access to course offerings, counseling and the use of appraisal and counseling materials, marital or parental status and athletics. *Marshall v. Kirkland*

*Section 504, The Rehabilitation Act of 1973* indicates that "No otherwise handicapped individual... will be excluded from the participation in, be denied the benefits of, or be subjected to discrimination under any program or activity receiving federal financial assistance solely because of his/her handicap. *School Board of Nassau Co v. Arline*

The *Age Discrimination Act of 1967* states that it shall be unlawful for an employer to fail or refuse to hire or discharge any individual or otherwise discriminate against any individual with respect to his/her employment because of an individual's age. This statute does allow an employer or employment to consider age as a bone fide occupational qualification (bfoq). *Geller v. Markham*

**Managing the School Climate in a Respectful and Inclusive Manner**

Administrators should be aware of the operation of the school grapevine and incorporate its positive aspects into the communication structure. The negative aspect of unsubstantiated rumor-passing will be overridden if the administrator consistently does the following:

- keeps employees informed about matters relevant to the school or district and about issues that impact the employees' jobs

- provides employees the opportunity to express attitudes and feelings about issues

- tests employees' reactions to information before making decisions

- builds morale by repeating positive reactions/comments made by employees to higher level administrators or the community and vice versa

Teaching professionals do not like the feeling that they are being kept in the dark or are getting only partial or untimely information. Telling teachers in a faculty meeting that the district is going to reduce the faculty at their school before transfer provisions have been established will create distrust. It may seem to be an open gesture on the principal's part, but the timing is wrong and such a communication will do more harm than good.

**Overcoming Barriers to Communication**

Filtering is a barrier that occurs during transmission of information from one level to another. It may be intentional or unintentional. It may be the omission of some of the message or improper encoding for the intended audience. Administrators frequently deliver information only on a need-to-know basis or deliver only positive information, fearing that negative information will damage the decoding process. This succeeds only in causing the receivers to be confused as to the message's intent or to feel patronized.

Biases against race, gender, or status can prejudice receivers against a message. Senders can suggest bias by words, nonverbal clues, or attitudes. A male principal with chauvinist attitudes may alienate female teachers; and a female principal may be tuned out by a male teacher who resents her. Unacknowledged biases frequently interfere unconsciously, underling the importance of developing cultural competence as noted earlier.

Overcoming these barriers is an important administrative responsibility. To establish effective communication, the school leader should:

- Establish trust by sincerely correlating his or her message and behavior. For example, claiming an open-door policy but never being available will not create trust.

- Listen carefully and provide open channels for feedback. Avoid giving non-verbal cues that contradict the message.

- Understand and respect employees' needs, interests, and attitudes. Allow discussion, even disagreement. The important thing is that employees know they are being heard.

- Properly time information delivery. Timing affects the manner in which employees perceive the message. Avoid leaking partial information. Transmit accurate information in time for employees to provide feedback.

- Use appropriate media for transmitting the message. Written or face-to-face communication is necessary when the message is of concern to a single receiver or when the message is of immediate concern to a group with common interests. Oral or video presentations are appropriate for delivery of information that affects a department or faculty, such as safety measures or procedures for reporting abuse.

**Summary of Good Communication Practices**

- Think first. This means preparing for a formal written, or oral presentation and it means pausing to gather your thoughts before impromptu speaking.

- Stay informed. Never speak or write off-the-cuff or attempt to discuss matters beyond your scope of knowledge. Stay abreast of education issues, especially in leadership and supervision. Read journals and participate in professional organizations. Keep a notebook of newsletters, clippings, and resource lists that can be highlighted and used to add credibility to your communication.

- Assess your audience. Know the addressees interests and attitudes. Show respect for their points-of-view by your tone and pace as well as by your volume and posture when speaking. Demonstrate a genuine liking for people by a willingness to share your ideas and solicit their responses.

- Focus attention on your message, not on yourself. A little nervousness is normal even for practiced writers/speakers. Familiarity with your topic, the ability to develop clear, complete sentences, and the use of concrete examples will enhance delivery.

- Speak/write correctly. Use of proper grammar, word-choice, and sentence structure will allow listeners/readers to concentrate on what you say, rather than on distracting language errors.

- Be concise. Get to the point and then quit. Use words and sentences economically. Being unnecessarily long-winded is a sure way to lose your audience.

- Use delivery techniques to your advantage. In written communication, be sure to state the main idea, give examples or explanations, and link the ideas in a logical manner. In oral communication, use eye contact to establish sincerity and hold listener attention. Use body language to add enthusiasm and conviction to your words, but avoid expansive or repetitive movements that can distract. Modulate the pitch and volume of your voice for emphasis.

Listen thoughtfully to feedback. In face-to-face communication, be aware of nonverbal cues that suggest either active listening or boredom.

Skill 3.7 Demonstrating knowledge of strategies for creating a positive, safe, and supportive learning environment for all students, including provision of student services (e.g., guidance) and activity programs to meet students' academic, athletic, cultural, developmental, leadership, and social needs

The role of the principal has changed significantly in the past ten years. Prior to this, principals were the managers of the school building: They made sure all aspects were working together according to specification. They ensured that activities were safe and cost effective, that all students had places to go during the day, that students were behaving properly, and that teachers had the resources they needed~~ to teach~~.

Lately, there has been a shift to thinking of principals as instructional leaders. They are expected to be thoroughly aware of each classroom, the instructional styles of each teacher, and the learning outcomes of all students. In summary, they are held responsible for the quality of instruction and the depth of learning at their schools.

With this shift of responsibilities~~, though~~, comes a dilemma for most school leaders: Should they focus on instruction at the expense of~~ all~~ other areas they know to be effective in the development of student growth~~, as well as the refinement of~~ and a positive school culture? Or do they try to balance both demands—which takes much more time, money~~cost~~, and effort?

Most principals would argue that both are necessary, no matter the cost. They realize that students, their families, and teachers need to see that all students' needs are met on a variety of levels. Schools are ideal places to provide various athletic, creative, and intellectual activities. Furthermore, these activities provide schools with a greater sense of community.

How do principals balance those two disparate roles, as well as facilitate the development, implementation, evaluation, and refinement of student services and activities~~y programs~~ to fulfill academic, developmental, social, and cultural needs?

First, principals must focus on the school's mission. Most schools think beyond test scores and student achievement in their mission statements. For example, a school that says that its mission is to prepare students to succeed in a changing world ~~will ultimately~~must acknowledge that achievement is important. However, such a school will also offer students opportunities to succeed socially, physically, and creatively. As school needs are identified ~~in order~~ to reach those broad goals, principals can ~~help~~ select faculty to participate and~~; they can also~~ set aside money. As they allocate school resources—money, personnel, time, and space—they must be ~~very~~ careful to ensure that students are treated fairly and equally. Today~~In this day and age~~, directing significant resources to the football team—and few resources to the chess team—may be seen as highly unfair.

In addition to activities, principals must ensure that unpredictable student services needs are met~~nimble and responsive to needs that may arise at random times~~. For example, a highly bureaucratic student services office may not respond quickly when emergencies arise and students—en masse—need counseling. Such offices also need to pay close attention to the requests of parents. Principals can help to assure this by instituting planning sessions and regular meetings to review policies, procedures, and school goals. Such staff should play critical roles throughout the campus so that they see the concerns and needs of teachers, as well as students when they are in academic and athletic environments.

Skill 3.8 Demonstrating knowledge of how to develop and implement effective behavior management approaches, student codes of conduct, and violence prevention practices and procedures

In 2004, the Florida Legislature signed into law House Bill 769 that amended several laws related to career and technical education. This was in response to goals to ensure that every Florida high school graduate is prepared to be successful in postsecondary education and the workplace. To successfully transition from middle school to high school and on to postsecondary education or the world of work, all students within the system must be supported by rigorous and relevant curriculum.

This bill also created Section 1006.025, Florida Statutes (Guidance Services) that requires district school boards to submit a guidance report to the Commissioner of Education by June 30 of each year. The guidance report must include the following:

- Examination of student access to guidance counselors

- Degree to which a district has adopted or implemented a guidance model program
- Evaluation of the information and training available to guidance counselors and career specialists to advise students on areas of critical need, labor market trends and technical training requirements
- Progress toward incorporation of best practices for advisement as identified by the department
- Consideration of alternative guidance systems or ideas, including, but not limited to, a teacher-advisor model, mentoring, partnerships with the business community, web-based delivery, and parental involvement
- Actions taken to provide information to students for the school-to-work transition
- A guidance plan for the district.

**School Discipline**

Principals are ultimately responsible for all school disciplinary measures. They must work with other school personnel to ensure that student behavior is monitored and managed in order to provide a safe and functional environment that encourages learning. In Florida, there exists a zero tolerance policy for crime, substance abuse and victimization of students. This policy is detailed in Florida statute 1006.12 (available at http://www.fldoe.org/safeschools/zero.asp).

A proactive approach can be very useful in preventing crime and victimization, and needs to be part of the overall plan for managing student discipline. One element of a proactive approach is establishing clear policies including but not limited to the following:

1. Weapons on school grounds
2. Homicidal and/or suicidal intent
3. Use of drugs and alcohol
4. Self-harm
5. Sexual harassment
6. Bullying
7. Violent threats

However, policies are not enough. Various prevention efforts can be effective in eclipsing student misbehavior, encouraging positive student interactions, and decreasing crime, violence and victimization in the school setting. Programs on bullying, sexual harassment and substance abuse need to be a regular part of the school curriculum.

Further, preventing violence and victimization is fundamentally related to resolving conflicts in interpersonal relations. Violence prevention efforts must be accompanied by programs of constructive conflict resolution so students can learn methods of positive interactions with others. Not only do these programs help create a safe environment in the schools, but they also teach students the skills to resolve future conflicts in their careers, family, and community as adults.

The National Youth Violence Prevention Resource Center offers resources on bullying and violence prevention and addresses substance abuse and other safety issues for teens at **www.safeyouth.org/scripts/topics/school.asp.** Other bullying and violence prevention resources are available at **www.cdc.gov/ncipc/dvp/YVP/YVP-data.htm, mentalhealth.samhsa.gov/15plus/aboutbullying.asp, and stopbullyingnow.hrsa.gov/index.asp.**

**Emergency Response Planning**

The best method of keeping students and staff safe is careful planning. It is crucial that all school community members are familiar with all emergency response plans. To ensure student and personnel safety, various levels of planning must be implemented. Plans must exist for ensuring safety in a variety of situations. Local natural disasters must be accounted for, as should plans for ensuring safety when, for example, the police are searching for a loose criminal in the surrounding neighborhood. Many schools may even have to consider safety plans for local terrorist attacks, particularly if the school is located near a busy or popular area.

Plans should include methods for getting students in a safe area, as well as communication among staff members and between administrative personnel and parents or media. Strategies for dealing with crisis reactions also need to be in place and are addressed in the next section (Crisis Management and Intervention Planning).

In planning for evacuation, routes should be drawn so that each hallway has the least amount of students walking through it possible, with no student having to walk too far. The quickest route out of a building may clog a hallway, thereby making the route much slower. However, it would also be unwise to have a whole classroom full of students walk far around a particular hallway and still be in a potentially dangerous location. Often, fire departments or safety consultants can assist in designing solid, quality evaluation plans.

A lock-down plan is the opposite of an evacuation plan, and consists of various rules and procedures for getting or keeping all students in a secure location, such as a classroom. Often communication suffers during a lock-down, so many schools now insist that school personnel look at their email accounts as soon as a lock-down occurs, to give the administration an efficient way to communicate to many people quickly.

The next level of ensuring safety concerns communicating those plans to staff, parents, students, and the district. Fire drills, for example, do not command great attention from most staff and students, typically because most people have never experienced a fire in a large institution. However, good administrators find creative ways to ensure that all staff members and students know the procedures. Clear directions should be posted all over campus for clarification when events occur. Directions and procedures should be mailed home to parents annually, as well.

When disasters or safety concerns occur, school leaders must behave like flight attendants: calm and collected, but decisive and clear. People in the school community will behave in a positive, productive manner during an emergency when the leadership gives clear instructions, is open and honest, and maintains a sense of peace while acting decisively.

After events that compromise safety, school leaders must do a few things. First, they must report all factors immediately to district administrators, local police, parents, students, and sometimes media. Second, they must sit down with other staff members and discuss the performance of the school community in responding to the crisis. From that discussion, the team can then make informed modifications to the plans. New plans, of course, must then be communicated to all stakeholders.

**Crisis Management and Intervention Planning**

Crisis and emergency situations such as those described above are events beyond the realm of every day life. They always involve some degree of surprise, shock, loss and emotion. The unpredictability of crises, the experience of loss that invariably accompanies such situations and the strong feelings that are evoked all make crisis and emergency events particularly potent and challenging for everyone involved. It falls on the shoulders of the building principal, in many cases, to manage the response to such traumatic situations.

Pre-planning and training in basic crisis management skills can be extremely helpful in responding effectively. Although the events themselves may be unpredictable, there is a body of information about how people react to crisis and what responders can do to ameliorate and manage the aftermath of crisis. This is important in school settings, where there are a large number of people congregated in one place and contagion is a concern. Anxiety and misinformation can spread like wildfire, exacerbating the short and long term effects of traumatic events.

Creating and training a crisis response team can be quite beneficial. Comprehensive crisis management training as well as ongoing refresher courses are necessary for a team to function well. A clearly designated leader (generally not the building principal who has enough to do in a crisis) should be chosen to head the team.

In addition to a crisis team, schools need to have clearly defined crisis response plans. They should include as much detail as possible, with specific recommendations for different situations as needed (as noted above regarding evacuation and lock-down), although a general plan is applicable in many circumstances. The plan should incorporate the following:

- delineate the school's goals in crisis situations (such as maintaining as normal a school day as possible, or providing timely information),
- identify key players on the crisis response team,
- specify how communication will be handled,
- describe what interventions will be used with students,
- note how interactions and referrals to outside agencies will be managed,
- detail what follow-up is needed.

Further, it helps to have handouts about traumatic stress reactions, sample letters to parents and guardians, press releases (when appropriate) and other useful documents ready prior to any event.

**Prescription Medications Policy**

The following statute addresses the administration of medication by school personnel to students. This is an example of the range of issues that principals face in attending to student needs on a day-to-day basis.

*Florida Statute 232.46* *Administration of medication by school district personnel.*

*Each district school board shall adopt policies and procedures governing the administration of prescription medication by school district personnel. The policies and procedures shall include, but not be limited to, the following provisions:*

*1. For each prescribed medication, the student's parent or guardian shall provide to the school principal a written statement which shall grant to the principal or the principal's designee permission to assist in the administration of such medication and which shall explain the necessity for such medication to be provided during the school day, including any occasion when the student is away from school property on official school business. The school principal or the principal's trained designee shall assist the student in the administration of such medication.*

*2. Each prescribed medication to be administered by school district personnel shall be received, counted, and stored in its original container. When the medication is not in use, it shall be stored in its original container in a secure fashion under lock and key in a location designated by the principal.*

*(2) There shall be no liability for civil damages as a result of the administration of such medication when the person administering such medication acts as an ordinarily reasonably prudent person would have acted under the same or similar circumstances.*

Skill 3.9 Recognizing broad principles for designing, implementing, and evaluating curriculum, instruction, and assessment for students at different educational levels (e.g., early childhood, middle school) and for students with diverse backgrounds and needs

It is important to address diverse student needs. Curriculum strategies must change according to the students' educational levels, i.e.: whether they are in early childhood, elementary, middle school, or secondary schools. Additionally, students will bring individual learning needs and diverse requirements to the educational environment. Administrators must be ready to meet the needs of all students and must therefore be prepared to address issues of diversity, subject-matter mastery, and developmental-level challenges. In order to prepare for these challenges, schools and districts frequently develop protocols created by panels of experts who specialize in different subject areas, educational levels, or areas of diversity.

For instance, a superintendant may convene a commission of representatives from various ethnic and cultural groups. School districts typically also have task forces to ensure that services are provided for students with special needs. No matter what segment of the population they represent, curriculum committees are ultimately responsible for adhering to best practices in curriculum development. They must, therefore, be well-informed of current learning theories, utilize contemporary practices in curriculum design, and be committed to educating all students to their fullest potential.

**GA Skill 5.1 Applies major principles, theories, and best practices of curriculum development and developmentally appropriate instruction**

The state-mandated standards must determine the nature and organization of the schools instructional aims, goals, and objectives. The standards should also dictate the subject matter, learning activities, and assessments. Curriculum design precedes instructional design. It is the phase concerned with the nature of the component parts, which is influenced by various philosophies, theories, and practical issues.

Before initiating the process, the designer must develop a blueprint by specifying the nature of each of the elements included in the design .The goals and objectives should be specific. In that way all those involved will clearly understand what will be taught and what behaviors are expected of the learner. The next step is to identify the resources needed to attain the preset goals and objectives for the curriculum. All material and human resources deemed necessary must be identified and secured. Materials might include textbooks, charts, maps, and sport equipment. Technology and equipment could be projectors, computers, calculators, and microscopes. Human resources include administrators, teachers, volunteers, support staff, and others. Facilities are classrooms, gymnasiums, athletic fields, cafeterias, and auditorium spaces. Educators must also determine the subject matter, methods of organization, activities, and methods and instruments of evaluation.

The organization of the components of the curriculum or the conceptual framework consists of two distinct organizational dimensions, which include horizontal and vertical organization. *Horizontal organization* is a typical side-by side course arrangement where the content of one subject is determined relative to the concepts of another related subject. For instance horizontal organization would involve planning a curriculum around global warming for 11th grade students. They would learn about the topic across various subject areas including mathematics, science, literature, and art. *Vertical organization* is concerned with longitudinal treatment of concepts within a subject across grade levels. Mathematical concepts are vertically organized when 11th grade students build on the knowledge they learned in 10th grade and then add to the knowledge in 12th grade. The success of the horizontal organization depends heavily on the collaboration of teachers of various disciplines at the grade level, while the vertical organization depends heavily on collaboration and planning among teachers of various grade levels.

The curriculum's dimensions are also determine its design. Therefore, attention should be given to curriculum scope, sequence, integration, continuity, articulation, and balance. *Curriculum scope* refers to the breadth and depth of the curriculum content at any grade level in terms of the content, learning activities and experiences, and topics. *Curriculum sequence* refers to the order of topics to be studied over time in a vertical dimension. The sequencing of the curriculum is usually organized from simple to complex learning, but it can also emphasize chronological learning, whole to part learning, or prerequisite learning. *Curriculum integration* refers to the linking of the concepts, skills, and experiences in the subjects taught. *Curriculum continuity* deals with the spiral or vertical smoothness of knowledge repetition from one grade-level to another in specific subjects or areas of study. *Curriculum articulation* refers to the interrelationship within and among subjects both vertically and horizontally. *Curriculum balance* refers to the opportunities offered for the learners to master knowledge and apply it in their personal, social, and intellectual life pursuits.

Curriculum content can be based on a number of different design principles. For example, *subject-centered* designs reflect the discipline-based approach to learning. The curriculum is organized according to essential knowledge that must be learned in the different subject matters.

The *discipline* design is based on the organization of content, which allows for in-depth understanding of the content and the application of meaning. It is used primarily in secondary schools to emphasize the organizational content inherent to the academic discipline such as science, math, English, etc. Thus, students in science, for example, would approach science as a scientist would. The emphasis becomes experiencing the discipline as learning takes place. In the *broad-fields design*, related subjects are broadened into categories, such as social studies encompassing history, geography, and civics or physical science encompassing physics and chemistry. This is unlike the subject-field design where a subject is studied separately from other subjects that are related, The intent of the broad-field design is to integrate the traditional subjects so that the learner develops a broader understanding of the areas included.

The *process-centered* design addresses how students learn and apply a cognitive process to the subject matter. This design focuses on the students' thinking process and incorporates procedures for children to advance knowledge.

Curriculum selection must also take into account contributions from the field of psychology, which is responsible for the major theories of learning. Learning theories serve as the foundation for methods of teaching, materials for learning, and activities that are age and developmentally appropriate for learning. It also provides the impetus for curriculum selection. Major theories of learning include behaviorism, cognitive development, and phenomenology or humanistic psychology.

*Behaviorism* represents traditional psychology, it emphasizes conditioning the behavior of the learner and altering the environment to obtain specific responses. As the oldest theory of learning, behaviorism focuses specifically on stimulus response and reinforcement for learning. The work of Thorndike led to the development of connectionism theories from which came the laws of learning:

> *Law of Readiness: when the conduction is ready to conduct, satisfaction is obtained and, if readiness is not present, it results in dissatisfaction.*
>
> *Law of Exercise: a connection is strengthened based on the proportion of the number of times it occurs, its duration, and its intensity.*
>
> *Law of Effect: responses accompanied by satisfaction strengthens the connection while responses accompanied by dissatisfaction weakens the connection.*

These laws also influenced the curriculum contributions of Ralph Tyler, Hilda Taba, and Jerome Brunner. Their view discarded the concept of specific stimuli and responses to endorse broader views of learning. For example, Taba recognized that practice alone does not automatically transfer to learning.

Jerome Bruner, on the other hand, contributed the notion that learning the structure provides a better basis for transferring learning than rote memorization. *Classical conditioning* emphasized learning as a response elicited through adequate stimuli. The most famous of these experiments was conducted by Pavlov. In it, a dog learned to salivate at the sound of the bell at which time food was presented simultaneously with the stimulus. From this came the notion that the learner could be conditioned for learning and thus be trained to become educated in any profession. *Operant conditioning* or behavioral theories were promoted by B. Frederick Skinner. These theories emphasize positive and negative reinforcers to determine behaviors. This is accomplished by either providing or withdrawing the stimuli or providing new operants. *Behavioral theories* gave birth to behavior-modification approaches to discipline and learning. Albert Bandura's theory of Observational Learning and Modeling focuses on children learning through modeling the behaviors of others. His theory contributed the notion that children's behaviors are shaped through observation of the behaviors of others. *Hierarchical Learning Theories* were promoted by Robert Gagne. They organize types of learning in a classical hierarchy encompassing intellectual skills, information, cognitive strategies, motor skills, and attitudes learned through positive experiences.

*Cognitive-development theories* focus on human growth and development in terms of cognitive, social, psychological, and physical development. The *Developmental Theory* of Jean Piaget is based on the supposition that growth and development occurs in stages. Piaget identified four stages of development including the sensory stage (birth to age two) in which the child manipulates the physical surroundings; the pre-operational stage (ages 2-7) in which complex learning takes place through experiences; concrete operation stage (age 7-11) in which the child organizes information in logical forms using concrete objects; and the formal operation stage (age 11 and above) in which the child can perform formal and abstract operations.

Phenomenology or humanistic psychology emphasizes the total organism of a person during the learning process, rather than separating learning into the domains of behavior and cognition. Some psychologist reject this school because they believe that psychology in-and-of-itself is humanistic in nature; therefore, there is no need for phenomenology. Gestalt psychology is representative of phenomenology and humanistic psychology. It represents wholeness as recognized in Maslow's Hierarchy of Needs, in which the end product is a wholesome, happy and healthy child/person who is self-actualized and fulfilled.

*Phenomenology or Humanistic psychology*, while not widely recognized as a school of psychology, is recognized by many observers as a third grouping. It emphasizes the total organism of a person during the learning process rather than separating learning into the domains of behavior and cognition. Psychology rejects this school because of the belief that psychology in-and-of-itself is humanistic in nature. Therefore, there is no need for such school. The *Gestalt psychology* is representative of phenomenology and humanistic psychology. It represents wholeness as recognized in Maslow's Hierarchy of needs in which the end product is a wholesome, happy and healthy child/person who has self-actualized and is fulfilled.

The school curriculum should satisfy societal needs and specific goals to produce individuals who have the social, intellectual, moral, emotional, and civic development to function as integral parts of our democratic society. Selecting the best curriculum to meet all of these needs is not an easy task; however, it can be facilitated thorough a collaborative approach. When program changes are necessary, there should be a clear rationale that examines the existing goals of the district and school. Clarification should be provided for the subjects, their structure and content, as well as the students' abilities, performance, and useful strategies. Consider the motivation of students and instructional staff, feasibility of time and resources, and curriculum balance in terms of concepts, skills, and applications.

Skill 3.10 Recognizing effective strategies for addressing broad student goals (e.g., encouraging lifelong learning, promoting critical-thinking skills), communicating high expectations, and accommodating students' diverse needs

**PX Skill 4.1 Knows major cognitive strategies associated with student learning**

**Skill 4.1 Knows major cognitive strategies associated with student learning**

Orela 3.10

Teachers should have a toolkit of instructional strategies, materials, and technologies to teach and encourage students to problem solve and think critically about subject content. When districts choose a curriculum, it is expected that students will master established benchmarks and standards of learning. Research of national and state standards indicates that there are additional benchmarks and learning objectives measured in all state assessments. These apply to most subjects including science, foreign language, English/language arts, history, art, health, civics, economics, geography, physical education, mathematics, and social studies. (Marzano & Kendall, 1996).

***Critical Thinking***

It is important that students develop critical thinking skills. When a student learns to think critically he/she learns how to apply knowledge to a specific subject area; but more importantly, the student knows how to apply that information in other subject areas. For example, in algebra, students must be taught the order of numerical expressions. To foster critical thinking, the teacher would teach the concept and then provide a math word-problem for students to compute the amount of material needed to build a fence around an 8' x 12' backyard. To solve the problem, students must think critically and group the fencing measurements into an algebraic word-problem and perform minor addition, subtraction, and multiplication to determine the amount of material needed. Their new skill could be applied to geography, science, woodworking, sewing, baking, and many tasks that are outside of the mathematics classroom.

As another example, students use basic reading skills to read passages, math word problems, or project directions. To fully comprehend the material read, however, students must apply additional thinking skills. These higher-order, critical thinking skills operate as students "think about thinking". Teachers are instrumental in helping students use these skills in everyday activities such as:

- Analyzing bills for overcharges
- Comparing shopping ads or catalogue deals
- Finding the main idea from readings
- Applying what's been learned to new situations
- Gathering information/data from a diversity of sources to plan a project
- Following a sequence of directions
- Looking for cause and effect relationships
- Comparing and contrasting information in synthesizing information

***Creative & Higher-Ordered Thinking***

To create the ultimate environment for creative thinking and continuous learning, teachers should use diversity in instructional strategies, engaging and challenging curricula, and the latest technologies. When teachers are innovative and creative they model and foster creative thinking in their students. Encouraging students to maintain portfolios from projects and assignments will allow them to make conscious choices to include diverse, creative endeavors that can be treasured throughout their educational journey.

Individualized portfolios are performance-based assessments that allow teachers to chart student's academic and emotional growth. Teachers can also use semester portfolios to gauge progress. This is particularly important for older students who are constantly changing their self-images and worldviews. Through a teachers guidance, students can master a concept and create a bridge connecting knowledge to application. When this happens,the teacher can share an enjoyable moment of higher level learning with the student.

Art can be incorporated into most subjects including reading, math, and science. Mental mind mapping, graphic organizers, and concept web guides that are all instructional strategies that teachers can use to guide students into deeper subject matter inquiry. Imagine fostering creativity in students that mimics that of German chemist Fredrich August Kekule; he looked into a fire one night and solved the molecular structure of benzene! By helping students understand the art of "visualization" and the creativity of discovery, teachers could sow the seeds towards the cure for AIDS, cancer, or reading difficulties.

Other important, life-long educational processes include developing effective note-taking skills, welcoming diverse perspectives, and appreciating the greatest computer on record, the human mind. In addition, teachers should train students to use math manipulatives, a technique for visual processing. Next, the process of journaling can help students understand their own learning. Lastly, when students present information to the class using posters and Power Point presentations, these can be powerful, creative methods of teaching and learning.

***Inductive and Deductive Thinking***

In deductive reasoning or learning, a teacher presents general concepts or principles and provides specific examples supporting the generalizations. Inductive reasoning occurs in the reverse: a teacher presents information or data and encourages students to hypothesize, identify patterns, draw conclusions, and then finally produce generalizations. This tends to involve students more deeply in the learning process. A teacher should choose the method based on the goals of instruction and the needs of the students.

For example, when mother is working in the kitchen, children conclude that a meal is coming soon; when parents put our coats on us, we believe that we are going outdoors. These conclusions are drawn not from one observation but from repeated ones. This is inductive thinking: observing particular occurrences and drawing conclusions. Deduction is the opposite. We begin with a conclusion, for example, *all men are mortal*, and support the statement with particulars: *Socrates died, Plato died, all the men we have ever known have died; therefore, all men are mortal.* Sometimes wrong conclusions are drawn on the basis of particulars. There are many legal cases where particular pieces of evidence have been used to find a person guilty in a court of law. However, later a significant bit of evidence, such as the person's DNA, proves that the conclusion of guilt was wrong. Drawing incorrect conclusions are also common when students use inductive and deductive reasoning; therefore, teachers must closely monitor this process for it to be a useful tool in helping students become critical thinkers.

***Memorization and Recall***

Understanding students' learning styles allows a teacher to share and target specific memorization techniques. These then help students absorb the large quantities of material they are expected to recall and master. For example, mnemonics incorporate rhymes and acronyms and are effective for visual learners. Mnemonics rely not only on repetition to remember facts, but also on associations between easy-to-remember constructs and lists of data. It is based on the principle that the human mind can more easily recall insignificant data when it is attached (in a logical way) to spatial, personal, or otherwise meaningful information. Kinesthetic learners use their imaginations to create mind-pictures of events and actions. In contrast, auditory learners rely on note-taking, review, and recitation to facilitate memorization and recall.

It was once considered a mark of extraordinary intelligence and learning to be able to recite long poems or long selections from books, particularly the Bible. However, simple memorization no longer has the place in education that it once did. Now students are expected to apply their knowledge in new and challenging tasks. Even so, the ability to memorize and recall principles and ideas (even text) is an important attribute of the learned person. Thus, the classroom teacher has an obligation to promote and develop these skills.

***Social Reasoning***

Social theory refers to the use of theoretical frameworks to explain and analyze social patterns and large-scale social structures. The goal of social reasoning is to see an issue from different perspectives, to understand social and ethical concerns surrounding an issue, and to be able to step back and view the issue as an historian would. A teacher can use questioning on a given issue to strengthen students' social reasoning abilities (e.g., What is the history of this issue and has it changed over time? How do diverse communities view this issue? What are some ethical questions surrounding this issue? Who benefits or is harmed by this issue? What can I (the student) do about this issue?)

Though many researchers consider social theory a branch of sociology, it is inherently interdisciplinary because it uses from and contributes to a plethora of disciplines such as anthropology, economics, theology, history, and many others. Social theory attempts to answer the question "what is?" not "what should be?" One should therefore not confuse it with philosophy or with belief.

***Representation of Ideas***

A visual representation of an idea or concept is a powerful instructional and learning tool. Through these aides, a teacher can provide strong connections and foundations for student understanding In turn, by producing a visual representation, a student demonstrates his/her understanding of the idea or concept. This ability is often critical in problem analysis and solving, as well as in creative pursuits where hard facts are absent and conceptualization is subjective.

In our society, we often think of ideas as being represented in words; however, this thinking needs to be expanded. There are so many other means and devices that are available to the teacher. For example, the old adage, "a picture is worth a thousand words" is, in fact, a truism. Students incorporate ideas much better if they have an opportunity to absorb them through more than one sense. For example, when learning a unit on drama or even literature, nothing substitutes for seeing one of Shakespeare's plays performed. Graphs, charts, photographs, paintings, drawings, and videos all represent an idea (or set of ideas).

**COMPETENCY 4.0 Understand the use of instructional best practices to promote student learning and how to design and implement comprehensive professional growth plans to help ensure effective teaching and learning.**



**Skill 5.2 Facilitate the implementation of sound, research-based instructional strategies, decisions, and programs in which multiple opportunities to learn and be successful are available to all students.**

Effective teachers plan for instructional delivery even if they have taught the same lessons before. They continue to improve their~~upon the~~ presentation by finding new or additional materials that~~to~~ brings new energy ~~in~~to the teaching and learning~~ process~~. As part of teaching, planning is a deliberate act that can be long-range, short range, formal, and informal.

Long-range planning, such as units or semester plans, takes into account milestones, standards, and major goals over a period of time. It takes into account the nature of the content to be covered, the process in which the content will be covered, the approaches to take at varying stages, the activities to be used as well as resources needed. Short-term planning consists of daily lesson plans, weekly or even monthly plans or units for instruction. Daily and weekly lesson plans are usually more detailed and specific, while unit plans can be more general and serve as the source of the daily lesson plans. Daily, weekly or unit written plans, grouping of students, instructional materials selection, activities for specific experiences to attain specific goals, student assessment, and the like are all part of the planning process

The formal aspect of planning has greater breadth and scope, which includes long-term and short-term written plans. The informal aspect of planning is continuous and includes teachers ideas' that emerge (1) as resourceful teachers gather materials they believe will be useful for learning, (2) as teachers consider varying experiences that could be used for specific students, (3) as they share ideas with other professionals, (4) and as they consider~~toy with~~ ideas on how to do things better. Whether long-term or short-term, effective planning begins with a goals and objectives specification for learning. Once the goals and objectives are specified, instructional strategies and materials should be selected, followed by the appropriate evaluation techniques to assess learning.

Instructional planning also involves organizing the students for learning. Whole group and small group instruction are beneficial in different ways. Whole group instruction is beneficial when the teacher is introducing new concepts and skills while small group instruction is recommended when teachers want to ensure that the student master the material or that thorough learning has taken place. Students may be placed in ability groups for short-term activities. Long-term ability grouping such as tracking should be avoided to allow children, who would have been place in regular track and higher college bound track, to benefit from each other by learning together.

Generally, teachers believe that ability groups save time and allow focusing on the specific collective needs of the students. However, ~~it is recognized that~~ approaches such as cooperative groups, ~~at all levels of schooling~~ where students of mixed ability work together, result in higher academic achievement at all levels of schooling. Other added benefits include improved time on task and increased interpersonal skills. Cooperative grouping as a dominant approach to instruction does not negate the need to use, on a short-term basis, homogeneous groupings to work with children within the classroom. The teacher must be careful that short-term ability groups remain as such and that the lower groups still receive high quality instruction.

Instruction should be clear and focused, beginning with an orientation to the lesson and instructional objectives presented to students in a language that they can easily understand. The relationship between the current lesson and previous lessons should be made. Key points should be emphasized, concepts defined with examples and non-examples, cause and effect relationships established, and careful attention given to learning styles through the use of appropriate materials and strategies for learning. Students should be provided ample time for guided and independent practice in the form of class work and homework, and strategies to develop higher level thinking skills are used.

Effective teacher expressions are key in the verbal aspect of instructional delivery. Enthusiasm and challenges that are clearly articulated are as important as the planned delivery of instruction of itself. Instruction, demonstrated through body language that expresses interest and caring, may also contribute to verbal effectiveness. The teacher should use good verbal skills for effective questioning to monitor understanding, to keep student focus, and to give feedback to reinforce learning progress.

Skill 4.2 Applying knowledge of theories and principles of human development, learning, and motivation to the learning process

## Skill 2.11 Applied motivational theories

The two most common motivational theories in education are intrinsic and extrinsic motivation.

**Intrinsic motivation** is when a person is motivated by internal factors, as opposed to external. Intrinsic motivation drives people to do things because they are fun or because they believe they are a good or right thing to do. Intrinsic motivation is a much stronger motivator than extrinsic motivation. Subject areas that become a student's passion are intrinsic motivators. Much learning at a young age is intrinsically motivated as children love school and learning new ideas and concepts. This motivation returns when students are older and have developed deeper knowledge and understanding of specific skills and concepts.

**Extrinsic motivation** is motivation by external factors. It drives people to do things for tangible rewards or pressures, rather than for the fun of it. Students are often motivated in school to try to please parents, be eligible for sports, or earn high marks for college admission. These are all examples of extrinsic motivators. Extrinsic motivation is often the impetus for learning during adolescence, at time when students develop ambivalence toward school and learning.

## Skill 2.12 Involvement of stakeholders in decision-making processes

The decision-making process includes a matrix of specialists who provide administrative direction in the school community. The Superintendent is the CEO of school communities and he or she hires principals to effectively lead individual schools. Principals must report to Secondary Executive Directors who are charged with the professional development and management of school leaders in the areas of school budgets, hiring and firing practices, evaluation of school staff, community communications, PTSA (Parent Teacher Student Association) collaborations, student programs, and a list of other duties as assigned.

A school's administrative team can consist of the principal, assistant principals, deans, activity/athletic directors and security. These individuals are all integrally involved in the decision-making processes that impact school communities. Schools make decisions on specific areas designated by school districts. Districts are the ultimate decision-makers in the school communities and each district has the active input of the School Board members.

Administrators must understand that there are various types of formal decision making processes that are implemented in school communities. Consensus is used by staff to actively vote on proposals of programs and curriculum. In consensus, the majority vote is used to determine if most of the staff is in favor of a proposal or implementation. Using a show of hands or written ballots provides the designated Union representative with a quantitative score to present to staff after a vote. In this format, the role of the administrator is to insure that the vote is accurate and carries a majority input of voters from the staff.

Other decision-making formats include Instructional Council votes that determine if curriculum designs are implemented during the current or upcoming school year. These councils are composed of department chairs for each academic core and program areas. They meet bimonthly to deal with issues such as registration, curriculum, staffing, and budget. In this format, the role of the administrator/principal is to facilitate effective and representative decision-making by the Instructional Council.

The Building Leadership Team is composed of staff volunteers, parent volunteers, and a student leader, who provides decision-making oversight of the building facilities and overall expectations of the academic subject areas. Administrators obtain decision-making input from this leadership team and then communicate decisions to the Instructional Council and the staff community.

When administrators serve on district interview teams, they must understand the expectations of them to make both subjective and objective decisions in hiring the best candidates for the positions.

Skill 4.3 Analyzing the significance of student diversity for teaching and learning



**Skill 3.9 Promote awareness of learning differences, multicultural awareness, gender sensitivity, and ethnic appreciation.**

As principals we are aware that a school with a variety of races, ethnicities, and learning differences can provide extraordinary academic and social opportunities to the entire school community. Diverse schools offer opportunities not always available in other settings. When knowledge can be shared not only by teachers and textbooks, but also by fellow students with a variety of life experiences and cultures, learning takes on a whole new meaning. For example, classroom discussions with students from varying backgrounds can be rich and challenging, fostering critical thinking skills. Students learn there are different perspectives on global issues, motivating them to study and more thoughtfully define their own views.

It is also important to make sure that everyone feels safe and comfortable in school. Try to make students and parents feel welcome and included in every aspect of the school community. Invite members of diverse groups to share their stories or cultures with others.

School principals must ~~learn to~~ recognize and respect the diversity in their school. The key for effective school leaders in a diverse school is to face any obstacles early on, tackle them with energy and creativity, and build a school culture based on a foundation of respect and high expectations. Creating awareness amongst the entire school community is an important step in the success of a diverse school. When doing this, principals should ensure that community stakeholders know that diversity is recognized and valued in their schools. Principals should offer resources, such as professional development, to help teachers and parents become more culturally aware. Additionally, principals should provide an environment where all stakeholders are treated fairly and equitably.

Skill 4.4 Demonstrating knowledge of how to use appropriate strategies and achievement data to profile student performance and analyze differences among subgroups



**Skill 5.5 Use formative and summative student assessment data to develop, support, and improve campus instructional strategies and goals.**

The evaluation of students is a very important aspect of the teaching and learning process. Periodic testing assesses learning outcomes based on the objectives established for learning and it provides information at various stages in the learning process to determine future learning needs such as periodic reviews, re-teaching, and enrichment. As the end process, the evaluation of students' performance measures the level of goal attainment achieved as a result of ~~, which is operationalized through~~ the learning activities planned by the teacher. At varying stages of the teaching and learning process, the intended outcome must be measured and the level of goal attainment is established in order to proceed with this continuous cycle of student evaluation.

Evaluation and measurement are often used interchangeably to imply the same process. However, while closely related, they should be differentiated. *Evaluation* is ~~identified as~~ the process of making judgments regarding student performance, and *measurement* is the actual data collection that is used to make judgments of student performance. Evaluation is related to student performance when ~~the focus is on~~ how well a student carries out a given task is measured or when a student's work or product is the focus of the measurement.

The purpose of the student evaluation will determine the type of process to use. Diagnostic evaluation, formative, and summative evaluations are the three types of student evaluations most commonly used. *Diagnostic evaluation* is provided prior to instruction to identify problems, to place students in certain groups, and to make assignments that are appropriate to their needs. While it is important to address the specific needs of students, teachers must be cautious of the ramifications of grouping children in homogeneous groups versus heterogeneous groupings. It may appear time effective to group and work with children of like situations, yet often it fails to foster students' intellectual and social growth and development. In fact, it has been proven that children in mixed groups benefit from the diversity within the group.

*Formative* evaluation is used to obtain feedback during the instructional process. It informs teachers of the extent to which students are really learning the concepts and skills being taught. The information obtained through the formative process should lead to modification in the teaching and learning process to address specific needs of the students before arriving at the end of the unit. Formative evaluation is designed to promote learning. Therefore, it must be done frequently using the specific objectives stated for learning outcomes. *Summative evaluation* is used to culminate a unit or series of lessons to arrive at a grade. It is the sum of all the accomplishments of the student over a specified period of learning. Knowing the content studied and having the specific skills required to score well on tests are two different endeavors which require not only learning content, but also following form.

Often, standardized tests are considered to be summative evaluations.

Therefore, it is also the responsibility of teachers to train the students in test taking skills with regard to following directions, managing time effectively, and giving special attention to the type of tests and the skills required.

Regardless of the type of assessment, educators must gather and analyze the information they yield to determine problem areas. The problem areas uncovered should be discussed with the students collectively and individually and also be presented as items for discussion at teacher conferences with parents. Whether diagnostic, formative or summative, the evaluation of student performance should be a continuous process.

The accuracy of student evaluation is essential. A~~The a~~ccuracy is related to consistency of measurement, which is observed through reliability and validity of the instruments used to measure student performance as well as usability of the instrument**.**

*Validity* is the extent to which a test measures what it is intended to measure. For example, a test may lack validity if it was designed to measure the creative writing of students, but it is also used to measure handwriting even though it was not designed for the latter.

*Reliability* refers to the consistency of the test to measure what it should measure. For example, the items on a true or false quiz, given by a classroom teacher, are reliable if they convey the same meaning every time the quiz is administered to similar groups of students under similar situations. In other words, there is no ambiguity or confusion with the items on the quiz.

*Usability* is another factor in the evaluation process, which refers to practical considerations such as scoring procedures, level of difficulty, and time to administer the test. The usability of a test will be questionable if the scoring procedures had to be changed to accommodate local financial circumstances or if the allotted time for the test had to be reduced because of other circumstances.

With the purpose of assessment instruments being one of data gathering, it is important to use various forms of information gathering tools to assess the knowledge and progress of students. Standardized Achievement Tests have become a central component of education today, particularly due to *No Child Left Behind*. The widespread use of standardized achievement tests to provide information for accountability to the public has driven many teachers to teach to the test and embrace more objective formats of teaching and learning. Although these tests are very limited in what they measure, too often they are used to make major decisions for which they are not designed.

Standardized achievement measurements can be norm-referenced or criterion-reference. In *norm-referenced* measurements the performance of the student is compared with the performance of other students who also took the same test.

The original group of students who took the test establishes the norm. Norms can be based on age, sex, grade level, geographical location, ethnicity, or other broad combination of classifications.

Standardized norm-referenced achievement tests are designed to measure what a student knows in a particular subject in relation to other students of similar characteristics. The test batteries provide a broad scope of content areas coverage so that it may be used on a larger scale in many different states and school districts. However, they do not measure the goals and content emphasized in a particular local curricula. Therefore, using standardized tests to assess the success of the curriculum or teachers' effectiveness should be avoided (McMillan, 1997).

Norm-reference standardized achievement tests produce ~~different types of~~ scores that are useful in different ways. The most common types of scores are the percentile rank or percentile score, grade equivalent score, stanine, and percentage of items answered correctly. The percentile score indicates how the students' performance compares to the norming group. It tells us that the percentage of the norming group was outscored by a particular student taking the test. For example, a student scoring at the eightieth percentile did better than 80% of the students in the norming group. Likewise, 20% of the norming group scored above the particular student and 80% scored below. The scores are indicative of relative strengths and weaknesses. A student may show consistent strengths in language arts and consistent weakness in mathematics~~ as indicated by the scores derived from the test~~. Yet one could not base remediation solely on these conclusions without a closer item analysis or a closer review of the objectives measured by the test. The grade equivalent score is expressed by year and month in school for each student. It is used to measure growth and progress. It indicates where a student stands in reference to the norming group. For example, a second grade student who obtained a grade equivalent score of 4.5 on the language arts section of the test is really not achieving at the fourth grade five month level as one may think. The 4.5 grade equivalence means that the second grader has achieved at about the same level of the norming group who is in the fifth month of the fourth grade, if indeed such a student did take the test. However, when compared to other second graders in the norming group, the student is about average.

A point of consideration with grade equivalence is that one may never know how well the second grader might do if placed in the fourth grade or how poorly the second grader might do if given the fourth grade test as compared to other second graders in the norming group.

Another type of standard score for standardized testing is the stanine, which indicates where the score is located on the normal curve for the norming group. Stanines are statistically determined but are not as precise as percentile ranking because it only gives the area in which the score is located, but not the precise location. Using stanines to report standard scores is still found to be practical and easy to understand for many parents and school personnel. Stanines range from one to nine (1-9) with five being the middle of the distribution.

Finally, achievement test scores can be reported by percentage of items answered correctly. This form of reporting may not be very meaningful when the items in a particular area are few. This makes it difficult to determine if the student guessed well at the items, was just lucky at selecting the right answers, or indeed chose the correct responses.

*Criterion-Referenced Standardized Achievement Tests* are designed to indicate the student performance that is directly related to specific educational objectives, thus indicating what the student can or cannot do. For example, the test may measure how well a student can subtract by regrouping in the tens place or how well a student can identify the long vowel sound in specific words. Criterion reference tests are specific to a particular curriculum, which allows the determination of the effectiveness of the curriculum, as well as specific skills acquired by the students. They also provide information needed to plan for future student needs. Because ~~of the recognized value of ~~criterion-referenced standardized achievement tests have recognized value, many publishers have developed tailor-made tests to correlate with state and districts' general goals and specific learning objectives by pulling from a test bank of field-tested items.

The test scores are reported by percentage of items answered correctly to indicate mastery or non-mastery.

*Aptitude tests* are another standardized form of testing that measure the cognitive ability of students. They also measure potential and capacity for learning. While they do not test specific academic ability, the ability level is influenced by the child's experiences in and out of the academic setting. Whether broad in measurement of the child's ability or focused, aptitude tests are used to predict achievement and for advanced placements of students.

*Teacher-made* tests are ~~also~~ evaluative instruments designed by classroom teachers to measure the attainment of objectives. While they ~~may~~ lack scientific validity, they serve the immediate purpose of measuring instructional outcomes. Teacher-made tests should be constructed to measure specific objectives, but they should also take into account the nature of the behavior that is being measured. Among teacher-made tests are multiple choice, essay, quizzes, matching, alternative choices (yes/no, true/false~~agree, disagree, and the like~~), and completion (fill in the blanks).

*Portfolio assessment* is fast becoming a leading form of teacher assessment, in which the student and teacher collect sample work in a systematic and organized manner to provide evidence of accomplishments and progress toward attaining specific objectives.

Certainly, testing is very important in the assessment of students' progress, but there are other sources of information that can be used for assessment. For example, conferencing can provide factual information for effective assessment, while the cumulative records of a child may also provide factual information for cognitive and psychomotor assessments. Other information sources may include interviews, diaries, self-assessment, observation, simulations, and other creative forms.

Skill 4.5 Demonstrating knowledge of strategies for supporting staff in understanding and applying best practices to enhance student learning



**Skill 3.1 Assessment of staff abilities and determination of their needs**

Career and staff development refers to the continual process of increasing the skills of professionals within the organization. Contemporary methods of staff development are extensive; however, there is sparse information on the actual impact of most methods. It is important to understand what works and what doesn't work when finding new ways to improve staff skills.

To differentiate the two, career development is deliberate training and practice meant to move a person into another career stage. For example, teachers who feel the call to school leadership typically go back to school, earn a master's degree, and become certified as a principal. Usually, this process takes place outside the K-12 school environment (teachers would attend university programs), however, some districts are experimenting with their own "in-house" training programs.

In contrast, staff development is meant to increase the skills of people in their current positions. So, while teachers may have been trained as in university-based certification programs, they will constantly need to be taught new strategies, skills, and techniques to use in their classrooms. Furthermore, good staff development helps to motivate teachers to further improve their practice.

The old model of staff development consisted of teaching discrete skills to teachers, often in impersonal large groups. Topics tended to be irrelevant to most teachers and there was no follow-up for teachers to discuss or reflect on new learning. Even though this is considered the "old" model of staff development, it is still used in many schools and districts across the country. Slowly but surely, schools and districts are learning that this model does not provide the impact needed to improve teacher practice and student learning.

The new model of staff development focuses on particular skills tailored to specific teacher needs. It includes significant follow-up time, sustained learning, and collaborative discussion. This model typically deals with individual subject areas or teacher techniques related to a particular grade level or subject. For example, instead of a session for all teachers in a high school, each department would learn things related to what they typically teach.

Additionally, the new model of staff development focuses on sustaining learning. Instead of providing teachers with a single training session, the topic is brought up throughout a school year. This might, for example, allow teachers to learn the strategy at the beginning of the year and try it for a few months. Then, half-way throughout the year, the topic can be discussed again in a staff development session. At that time teachers can learn new strategies to deal with problems they encountered during the "trial" period. Later in the year, teachers can get together and further reflect on the strategy and plan how they will use it in the coming year.

Staff needs and satisfaction should be surveyed on a regular basis. During the school improvement process, staff development needs should be identified and included in the plan to help acquire funding and other resources as necessary. Staff should be surveyed at least once per year to determine their interests, weaknesses, and preference for development. Many schools now have staff development committees that represent the entire staff and assist the administration in the planning of developmental activities. Each development session should also conclude with an evaluation to determine the usefulness of the session.

### Skill 3.2 Establishment of staff development priorities

Professional development is a crucial component of successful school change. New standards and accountability systems demand much more of teachers than ever before, and many teachers simply do not have the skills or knowledge to implement the many requirements for which they are now responsible.

Significant research on professional development has concluded that among the worst ways of helping teachers learn new skills or knowledge is by putting them through a "one-shot" staff in-service. A staff in-service is a session that focuses on a particular strategy or technique for the classroom. Sometimes, these sessions are one to two hours. Other times, they are five to six hours. In either case, these sessions give teachers no reason to utilize their new learning, nor do they take into account adult learning theory. Adult learning theory suggests that adults learn best when they have an immediate application of their learning. Since most staff in-services have no follow-up (i.e., discussion about how the strategy worked, one-on-one coaching, etc.), most teachers will not try the new strategies. After all, they feel safe and comfortable with their current procedures.

Effective professional development consists of deep learning across time with significant opportunities for follow-up, discussion, assistance, and reflection. Often, when professional development sessions, on one topic, are spread out over a whole year (perhaps, one three-hour session per month), teachers have more reason to follow through with trying new ideas in the classroom.

When schools add components of Professional Learning Communities—group configurations that allow for discussion of new learning—then teachers have more opportunity to reflect upon, discuss, and question the new ideas. This allows teachers to work through personal concerns and problems they might be facing in their classrooms.

Consistently, teachers report in surveys that they never have enough time to learn new strategies. Therefore, it is crucial that professional development not be limited to just a couple hours per year. Schools must provide teachers with multiple opportunities, often by re-arranging the school day, so that teachers can interact with each other and with new teaching ideas on a more regular basis.

Funds for professional development are critical, as well. While grants are often available, principals must be creative in providing teachers with the resources they need to be effective. If teachers do not get these professional development resources, it directly impacts student learning. As such, principals must view allocation for professional development as a necessity—not as a financial burden.

Skill 4.6 Applying knowledge of methods for promoting adult learning and developing professional growth plans for self and staff that reflect a commitment to lifelong learning and best practice

TX Skill 6.7 Engage in ongoing professional development activities to enhance one's own

**Skill 6.7 Engage in ongoing professional development activities to enhance one's own knowledge and skills and to model lifelong learning.**

~~The school~~Today's principal ~~today~~ is recognized as a critical person for impacting instructional change and bringing to fruition the goals and objectives of a school. The kind and quality of leadership exercised by those invested with the authority to supervise school operations makes a difference in the lives of students, the community, and ultimately the nation. Hence, the role of the principal and the competencies that an individual brings to this position are key elements in creating dynamic and effective school organizations.

There are various approaches to understanding the qualities of good leaders, qualities that principals may want to emulate. The trait approach to leadership focuses on the personality traits of leaders. The situational approach postulates that leadership is a result of understanding the idiosyncrasies and characteristics of specific groups. Additionally, research from Ohio State University places~~d~~ leadership in two dimensions, task and consideration. This two-factor view of leadership increases~~d~~ understanding of leadership behavior. Finally, ~~another approach to understanding leadership emerged, known as~~ the contingency approach~~. The contingency approach~~ specifie~~d~~s that the kind of leadership to be exerted depends upon a number of variables, including personality, task, group dynamics, and the situation.

Many theorists have proposed frameworks in an attempt to understand the dynamics that take place in organizations. Educational administration has borrowed extensively from organizational theorists to form a foundation. Early organizational theorists were more concerned with how well people performed given tasks in the enterprise than with the well being of the individuals in the organization.

These theories and beliefs about organizations and individuals were soon challenged by another set of theories and beliefs, which focused on the quality of relations and the importance of people in the organization. This evolutionary pattern continued, followed by critical analysis of the formal and informal structures existing in organizations. The conceptualization of organizations as a system, with internal and external influences, further contributed to the base of knowledge for educational administration and leadership.

A particularly salient view of leadership within organizations was developed by Bolman and Deal, 1997. They~~ir view is~~suggest that people within organizations operate within one (or more) of four organizational frames: structural, human resources, political, and symbolic. These authors argue that most leaders operate in the structural frame (focusing on hierarchies, rules, regulations, procedures, etc.) or the human resources frame (focusing on the needs of people; within schools, this could either be teachers, students, or both). The authors also argue that the two other frames, often ignored, are highly important for the proper running of an organization. The political frame focuses on sources of power, and the symbolic frame focuses on the symbols of organizational culture and history that are so important to employees, students, and others.

Ours is a rapidly changing world, which impacts the way organizations function. Moreover, changing situations require leaders of organizations to assess their abilities and to understand the characteristics needed to effectively lead their organizations (Lewis, 1993). It is apparent that school administration parallels that of business organizations and other enterprises in American society. The responsibilities of fiscal management, curriculum development, physical plant management, employee supervision, and personnel administration all require an administrator who possesses broad skills and knowledge (Rebore, 1998). Furthermore, within our age of school accountability, schools need leaders who know how to effectively improve the instructional quality of their schools.



**SKILL 6.1 Work collaboratively with other campus personnel to develop, implement, evaluate, and revise a comprehensive campus professional development plan that addresses staff needs and aligns professional development with identified goals.**

Career and staff development refers to the continual process of increasing the skills of professionals within the organization. ~~In this day and age, t~~The methods of staff development are extensive; however, the evidence of impact of most methods is sparse. It is important to understand what works and what doesn't work when finding new ways to improve the skills of school staff members.

Let us first differentiate between career and staff development. Career development is deliberate training and practice meant to move a person into another career stage. For example, teachers who feel the call to school leadership typically go back to school, earn a master's degree~~,~~ and ~~become~~principal certification~~ed to be a principal.~~ Usually, this process takes place outside the schooling organization (at universities), although ~~however,~~ some districts are experimenting with their own "in-house" training programs.

Staff development, the domain typically of school districts themselves, is meant to increase the skills of people already in current positions. So, while teachers may have been trained as teachers in certification programs, they will constantly need to be taught new strategies, skills, and techniques to use in their classrooms. Furthermore, good staff development helps to motivate teachers to improve their practice further.

The old model of staff development consisted of teaching discrete skills to teachers, often in impersonal large groups. ~~Often, s~~Staff development topics have often been~~were~~ irrelevant to most teachers, and ~~;~~ typically~~, they had~~included no follow-up for teachers to discuss or reflect new learning. Even though this is considered the "old" model of staff development, ~~it is still used~~ they persist in many schools and districts across the country. Slowly but surely, schools and districts are learning that this model does not ~~provide the impact needed to~~ improve teacher practice and student learning.

The new model of staff development focuses on specific skills tailored to specific teacher needs. It includes significant follow-up time, sustained learning, and collaborative discussion. This model is specific in that it typically deals with individual subject areas or teacher techniques related to a particular grade level or subject. For example, instead of teaching all teachers in a high school about a particular technique, each department would learn things related to what they typically teach.

Additionally, the new model of staff development focuses~~ a lot~~ on sustaining learning. Instead of providing teachers with a single training session, the new model of staff development encourages ~~that the~~continual study of a topic ~~is brought up a few times~~ throughout a school year. This might, for example, allow teachers to learn the strategy at the beginning of the year so that they can try it out for a few months. Then, possibly half-way throughout the year, the topic can be brought up again in a staff development session, so that teachers can learn new strategies to deal with some of the problems they have experienced with it in their "trial" period. Later in the year, teachers can get together and further reflect on the strategy and plan out how they will use it in upcoming years.

**Skill 6.2 Facilitate the application of adult learning principles and motivation theory to all campus professional development activities, including the use of appropriate content, processes, and contexts.**

Motivation is defined by Baron (1992) as a force that energizes, sustains, and channels behavior toward a goal. Theorists maintain that there are two types of motivation. One is intrinsic motivation, which results from an individual's internal drive state and provides impetus toward goal attainment. The other is extrinsic motivation,~~ meaning that the orientation~~which uses external incentives and rewards to motivate~~ toward~~ goal achievement~~ is influenced by incentives and rewards external to the individual~~. Providing for the needs, desires, and preferences~~likes~~ of individuals in an organizational setting influences motivation and impacts the objectives of the organization. Motivating individuals is a complex process of trying to facilitate desired motivational patterns (Hoy & Miskel, 1996). A number of theories have been developed to explain what influences individuals to work enthusiastically, to want to engage in professional growth, to contribute to goal attainment in organizations, and to act responsibly.

Organizations have goals and objectives~~, which~~ they seek to achieve.~~ For the most part,~~ ~~t~~Th~~e~~ose goals and objectives ~~are achieved through~~depend on people facilitating them. The question of how to get people motivated to achieve those goals and objectives, expeditiously and effectively, is at the heart of motivational theories. Theories of motivation are grouped into the categories of *behavioral, cognitive*, and *humanistic.* The behavioral approach to motivation suggests that motivation depends upon the effectiveness of rein~~-~~forcers. Using~~The utilization of~~ specific rein~~-~~forcers to influence behavior ~~then becomes~~is an important element in the behavioral approach.

Cognitive theory suggests that there are two personal factors to consider in relation to motivation—expectations and beliefs (Eggen & Kauchak, 1997). ~~Those factors are expectations and beliefs.~~ When there is the expectation that one can succeed at a task, and value to achieving that task is attached, then a feeling of self-efficacy emerges. In organizations~~ then~~, leaders may ask what can be done to ~~help bring about emotions of~~increase a sense of self-efficacy in its members.

The Humanistic perspective views motivation as attempts by people to reach their potential (Eggen & Kauchak, 1997). Motivation proceeds from internal mechanisms that~~acting to~~ cause individuals to achieve, grow and develop, and reach their potential.

Incentives and rewards are used by an organization to ~~influence~~ motivate individuals~~'~~ ~~motivation~~ to be more productive ~~members in the organization~~. Of importance in any work environment are the environmental factors present, those things that tend to make the workplace enjoyable ~~and those things that tend to make the workplace~~or distasteful. Administrators' attentions to the factors, (which will permeate the workplace and, subsequently, have impact on the motivation of organizations' members to accomplish tasks) have a bearing on the fulfillment of organizational goals. Because individuals have needs, desires, likes, and dislikes and these are related to their motivation, an understanding of this and how it relates to work is important for the leadership function.

Currently, educational policy has relied on the idea of external motivation to improve instructional quality. *No Child Left Behind* operates largely on the principle that rewards and punishments will increase motivation levels of teachers, principals, and students. While growth targets are incremental, when they are not met, schools and staff may, for example, be transferred to other schools in the district. We may not know until 2014, when all students are expected to be fully proficient, how effective external motivation is for improving the learning of all students across the country.

**Skill 6.3 Allocate appropriate time, funding, and other needed resources to ensure the effective implementation of professional development plans.**

Professional development is a crucial component of successful school change. New standards and accountability systems demand ~~so much~~ more of teachers than ever before, and many teachers simply do not have the skills or knowledge to implement the many things they are not responsible for.

Significant research on professional development has concluded that among the worst ways of helping teachers learn new skills or knowledge is by putting them through a "one-shot" staff in-service. A staff in-service is a session that focuses on a particular strategy or technique for the classroom. Sometimes, these sessions are one to two hours. Other times, they are five to six hours. In either case, these sessions give teachers no reason ~~utilize~~ to apply their new learning, nor do they take into account adult learning theory, which ~~. Adult learning theory~~ suggests that adults learn best when they have an immediate application to their learning. Since most staff in-services have no follow-up (i.e., discussion about how the strategy worked, one-on-one coaching~~, etc.~~), most teachers don't~~will not~~ try the new strategies. After all, they feel safe and comfortable with their current strategies.

Effective professional development consists of deep learning across time with significant opportunities for follow-up, discussion, assistance, and reflection. Often, when professional development sessions~~,~~ on a~~one~~ topic~~,~~ are spread out over a whole year (perhaps, one three hour session per month), teachers have more reason to follow through ~~with~~and try~~ing~~ new ideas in the classroom. When schools add components of Professional Learning Communities—group configurations that allow for discussion of new learning—then teachers have more opportunity to reflect, discuss, and question the new ideas. This allows teachers to work through personal concerns and problems they might be facing in their classrooms.

Consistently, teachers report in surveys that they never have enough time to learn new strategies. Therefore, it is crucial that professional development not be limited to just a couple hours per year. Schools must provide teachers with multiple opportunities, often by re-arranging the school day, so that teachers can interact with each other and with new teaching ideas on a more regular basis.

Funds for professional development are critical, as well. While grants are often available, principals must get creative about providing teachers with the resources they need to be effective teachers. If teachers do not get these professional development resources, it directly impacts student learning. As such, principals must view allocation for professional development as a necessity—not as a financial burden.

Skill 4.8 Demonstrating knowledge of how to use various techniques (e.g., mentoring, conferencing) to promote new knowledge and skills among staff and how to encourage staff leadership, initiative, innovation, and reflection

See Georgia guide



**Skill 3.8 Instructional staff assessment, including conferencing, observation, data collection, and documentation of performance**

Appraisal of personnel is a significant part of a principal's responsibility. Most districts use district-wide criteria developed through a diverse committee of school-community representatives. These criteria provide the principal with objective and reliable methods of appraising staff. Teachers are also aware of the criteria and understanding how they are used in evaluations. Gossip, unsigned notes, and other such techniques are deemed unreliable and should not be used.

In evaluating building-level staff, principals must know the district's criteria. For many teacher evaluations, states require performance-based assessments; therefore, the principal must tie performance to student learning. If the principal needs to acquire additional information on the development and implementation of the appraisal process, he or she can contact district or state officials, university professors, professional organizations, or consultants.

In an effort to support teacher success, the state or district may provide assistance to new and experienced teachers new to teaching in the state. The assistance of a peer teacher and a variety of induction activities enable teachers to receive assistance without the implied threat of evaluation. This open system allows these teachers to seek help when it is needed.

When the evaluation process is conducted properly, teachers grow professionally and students benefit from increasingly effective instruction. Teachers should set professional-development goals based on weak areas and should receive recognition for areas of strength. The processes for gathering the data used to rate teachers should also be published and discussed. Most often, there are formal, planned classroom observations, as well as informal walk-throughs and other informal methods for viewing a teacher's work.

Teacher performance ratings should be directly tied to student achievement, so student achievement data should be included in determining appraisal scores. The driving motto should be that teaching has not happened unless students have learned! Teachers should be given clear feedback about whether their performance is adequately satisfying the criteria of the appraisal instrument. Delivering this feedback to the teacher in a face-to-face conference allows the appraiser to establish a dialogue with the teacher about instructional practices. Very few professionals change simply because someone talks to them, this includes teachers. To change behavior, administrators must change the thinking behind the behavior. This can be achieved by asking questions that cause teachers to reflect on their own practices.

As a principal, your goal is to improve your staff so that student achievement will be optimized. You will encounter underperforming teachers who are in need of assistance. With these individuals, agree on two or three improvement goals and concentrate on making progress in these areas before moving on to other areas of need. Document the improvement plan andany progress, or lack of progress, toward the selected goals. Poorly trained teachers need to observe excellent role models, so allow release time for observations in other classrooms. Conferencing with the mentee after the observation will assist them in applying what they observed in their own classroom. When a teacher is working through an improvement plan, the principal should make more frequent visits to the classroom and look for signs of improvement. Document every visit and intervention. Ineffective teachers can improve with a principal's support, training, and mentoring.

The appraisal process is also a way to provide recognition for outstanding teachers. When a teacher's performance is highly rated, this provides encouragement to continue instructional practices that benefit students.

Appraisal systems allow for the structured feedback that teachers need to improve instruction and grow professionally.

**Skill 3.9 Staff are treated fairly, equitably, and with dignity and respect**
ORELA 9.1

All staff need and deserve to be treated with respect, whether they are part of the teaching staff or the custodial staff. Staff members need to know that the administration is there to help in any situation, will respect confidential information, and does not show favoritism. Aspects of dealing with members of the staff include:

- Interpersonal communication
- Retention of staff
- Civility
- Reward and recognition
- Developing teams
- Establishing trust
- Managing stressful situations
- Supporting staff in times of change

When a new administrator comes into a school, he or she has to develop a sense of trust with the staff. They need to know that the administrator will support them in cases of problem students or if problems arise with parents. Staff who do an exceptional job need to be recognized and this should be done publicly such as at staff meetings. The administrator should look for exemplary teaching or behavior in all staff, but at the same time rewards and recognition should not be handed out frivolously.

Team-building is important in schools but it will take time. The administrator has to make sure that the members of the team get along. Teams with members who cannot work together will not function effectively. An administrator also has to be able to manage stressful situations without panicking or becoming distraught. This will let the teachers know they have a leader on whom they can depend. At the same time, the administration has to support the school district in bringing in policies and programs with which teachers may not agree. Therefore there will be times when teachers will be forced to change. The administrator has to realize that change is not easy and that teachers should be coached to take small steps leading to change.

Skill 4.9 Applying knowledge of various supervisory models (e.g., clinical, coaching) and effective faculty and staff evaluation procedures

See Georgia guide

**Skill 9.3 Uses a variety of supervisory models to monitor and improve instruction**

The vision of any school should be to provide effective instruction for students. To ensure that this takes place on a consistent basis, supervisors must work with teachers in a non-threatening way. Together, they can move instruction from what it is to what it should be.
Personnel appraisal is a significant responsibility for the principal. Done correctly, teachers grow professionally and students benefit from increasingly effective instruction. Most school districts provide district-wide, objective measures to judge teacher effectiveness. These are published and should be discussed with each teacher early in the school year. For instance, at the beginning of the term, teachers should set professional development goals. They should include both areas in which they are weak and those in which they are strong. A supervisor and his/her staff can then work collaboratively to achieve these goals. There are several methods of supervision that can be used:

**CLINICAL SUPERVISION:** Supervisors work with teachers in a collaborative way and provide expert, direct assistance. As the father of clinical supervision, Cogan believed that for this method to be effective, data had to be collected from the teacher in the classroom. Then, the supervisor and teacher involved would collaborate to plan programs, procedures, and strategies aimed at improving the teacher's classroom behavior, specifically his/her instructional techniques.
There are five phases in clinical supervision. The first is the planning conference or pre-conference, involving the supervisor and teacher. This session focuses on the reason and purpose for the observation, the focus of the observation, the method and form of observation to be used, the time of observation, and the time for the post-conference.

The second phase of the clinical supervision is the actual observation of the teacher in the classroom. During this time, data are collected based on what the supervisor has decided he/she would observe. Once the data are collected, analyses and interpretations are made. This is the third phase, which also involves deciding what approaches are to be used in the fourth phase.
The fourth phase, post-conferencing, focuses on reviewing the results of the observational session and formulating plans which will aid in improving future instruction. During the post-conferencing critique, the supervisor and teacher analyze the first three phases of clinical supervision, and make adjustments where necessary. This conference, not necessarily a formal one, examines questions such as: what was valuable in what we did and what changes in strategies can be made?

Clinical supervision allows for objective feedback, which if given in a timely manner, will lead to improved outcomes. As a result, teachers are able to clearly see differences in what they think they are doing and what they are actually doing.

**DEVELOPMENTAL SUPERVISION:** Teachers have different job skills, knowledge, behaviors, attitudes, and concerns at different points in their careers. A number of these characteristics follow a regular developmental pattern. Three stages of teacher career development have been identified, each with different developmental characteristics.

The survival stage occurs during the first year of teaching. At this stage, the teacher's major concern is meeting professional responsibilities and adjusting to the school environment. The confusion and uncertainty of the first stage can be allayed by direct supervisory assistance, with the supervisor assuming primary responsibility in helping the teacher.

The second, third, and fourth years of teaching are years of adjustment, growth in classroom techniques, and increasing confidence. A collaborative supervisory approach is appropriate at the adjustment stage, with the supervisor and teacher taking equal responsibility for meeting the teacher's needs.

At the mature stage, from the fifth year on, most teachers feel professionally secure. During the mature stage of teaching, stress is placed on the teacher's ability to keep his/her instruction interesting while meeting changing educational expectations. A nondirective, supervisory approach is appropriate at this stage. The supervisor listens, encourages, clarifies, presents, and collaboratively solve problems, while the teacher assumes the primary responsibility for improving instruction through self-assessment.

**COACHING:** Cognitive coaching is a framework based on the premise that teachers have the capacity to reflect upon their teaching and self-direct their actions based on new information brought forth through work with a coach. Through a deliberate and focused series of questions in a conference, a coach can lead a teacher to a different level of thinking, and therefore, better practice in the classroom. Coaches help teachers discern the healthy things they want to do or to be and find appropriate behaviors to get there. The coach and teacher are essentially peers, not "master and student."

Coaches believe that knowledge is within the teacher or within the teacher's grasp if he or she knows where and how to obtain it. Coaching is not focused on giving new knowledge or skill sets, but rather on the action plan for obtaining that knowledge or skill. The coach may point to various resources, but the initiative rests with the teacher to follow through. The coach and teacher "design an alliance" concerning what will be accomplished, but the teacher sets his or her agenda. The teacher and coach agree and work together to honor it. Coaching is oriented toward next steps and focuses on what behaviors will help the teacher reach his/her goals. The coach will also help the teacher deal with feelings so that they do not block the teacher's future goals. Finally, the coach keeps personal opinions and advice out of the conversation so that the teacher can move ahead on the agenda. Coaches must listen deeply and ask probing questions.

**COMPETENCY 5.0 Understand how to manage the organization at the school and district level in ways that promote learning and achievement and help ensure the success of all students**

Skill 5.1 Applying knowledge of learning, teaching, student development, organizational development, and data management to optimize learning for all students



**Skill 4.1 Facilitate effective campus curriculum planning based on knowledge of various factors (e.g., emerging issues, occupational and economic trends, demographic data, student learning data, motivation theory, teaching and learning theory, principles of curriculum design, human developmental processes, legal requirements).**

Program effectiveness can only be measured through the process of evaluation. Program evaluation is the process of collecting and analyzing data to discover whether the design, development or implementation is producing the desired outcomes. The data gathering and analyses also carry the purpose of making informed decisions about the program. It may lead to changing or eliminating aspects of the program.

The CIPP (Content, Input Process Product) model developed by Daniel Sufflebeam is an example of program evaluation. ~~In a three-step process,~~ ~~I~~Information ~~is provided~~ for decisions~~,~~ is provided in a three-step process, which includ~~ing~~es delineating the information to be collected, obtaining the information, and providing the information to others. These steps must then correspond with four distinct types of evaluation: content, input, process, and product evaluations (Onstein and Hunskin 1993). *Content Evaluation* is concerned with the environment of the program in terms of needs and unmet needs. *Context evaluation* constitutes the diagnostic stage of the evaluative process. It provides baseline information related to the entire system of operation. *Input Evaluation* is concerned with providing information and determining how to utilize resources to attain the goals of the program. It focuses on whether the goals and objectives for the program are appropriate to the expected outcome or if the goals and objectives are stated appropriately. It also takes into account whether the resources to implement specific strategies are adequate, whether or not the strategies are appropriate to attain the goals, or if the time allotted is appropriate to meet the objectives set forth for the program.

*Process Evaluation* focuses on decisions regarding curriculum implementation. It is concerned with whether the activities planned are being implemented and with the logistics of the total operation so that procedures are recorded as they occur and monitoring is continuous to identify potential problems. The continuous process of identifying potential problems leads to decisions to make corrections before or during the implementation of the program. For example, it might be necessary to establish special planning sessions or teacher in-service at specific grade levels to work on modification of some of the strategies established for the program because of problems uncovered. Process evaluation is also known as the piloting process prior to the actual implementation of a school-wide or district-wide program (Ornstein and Hunskin, 1993). Finally, *Product Evaluation* takes into account whether the final product or curriculum is accomplishing the goals or objectives and to what degree.

At this point decisions must be made regarding the continuation, termination or modification of the program. Since the evaluation process is continuous, at this point the evaluators may~~, at this point in the cycle,~~ link specific actions back to other stages of the cycle or make changes based on the data collected. The data obtained may very well indicate the need to delay full implementation of the program until such time that corrections are made, or it may lead to the decision that the program is ready for large scale implementation.

In summary, the main purpose of the evaluative process is to diagnose strengths and weaknesses, and to provide feedback to make appropriate decisions for programs and schools. The data collection for the evaluation process originates from a number of sources, including classroom observation, interviews and discussions with students, discussion with teachers and parents, testing and measurement data, information from pupil services or guidance services, and surveys of the school and school community.

Systematic assessment of school needs may range from grade level surveys of needs to school-wide surveys. This practice is insignificant, unless careful attention is given to a cohesive set of goals that are developed jointly with administrators, teachers, parents, and members of the school community to address specific needs. It is important that the instrument gathers pertinent information related to students‘ needs and the program situation at the school. Once the instrument is administered and the results are quantified, analyzed, and interpreted, the direction to follow is then determined.

When the purpose of the needs assessment is for program development, goal statements are carefully stated and established, and goals are prioritized and linked to performance outcomes of the learner. High priority goals are placed into a plan of implementation with specific strategies delineated. However, if the purpose of the assessment is for a progress check~~, then~~ the assessment instrument should reflect statements concerning activities and functions of the students and the staff, as well communication between the various levels. The systematic assessment of school needs should go beyond surveys to include cumulative folder content, anecdotal records, test results, interviews, classroom sociograms, direct teacher observation, and other means deemed appropriate.

Change is often~~, generally, desirable~~necessary for growth and development, but not all reasons
for change are plausible.  In many instances, the acceptance of change is dependent on concrete measures of comparison between the existing and the desired programs.  Such comparison might be done through the Purvus Discrepancy Evaluation Model in which program standards and performance must first be determined, then both performance and standards are compared to determine if indeed there are discrepancies. The discrepancy between standards and performance is established throughout every aspect of the program including the design, installation, processes, products and cost.

Whenil~~e~~ change is necessary, it will not occur just because someone has the knowledge for a bright idea that may very well be beneficial and~~ may~~ work beautifully. Change will occur when the individuals at all levels in the organization recognize that there is a need for it. It takes effective leadership and open two-way communication to initiate the change process. Problem solving, support, and continuous assessment of the process are also important aspects of promoting change.

The process of educating students is accomplished through instruction~~ that is~~ designed to attain specific objectives~~ that are~~ reflected in the educational aims and goals. Change occurs because the~~ people such as~~ principal, curriculum leaders, teachers, parents, staff, and students work together and~~by~~ accept~~ing~~ their roles as agents of change. The organizational pattern and climate must be transformed~~ in order~~ to accept change.

Skill 5.2 Demonstrating knowledge of skills for managing the organization with attention to indicators of equity, effectiveness, and efficiency, and for deploying financial and human resources to promote student achievement

**PRAXIS Skill 4.9 Sources, acquisition, and distribution of financial resources**

**Skill 4.9 Sources, acquisition, and diotribution of financial resources**

ORELA 5.2

There are three major sources of school funding for school districts. Approximately 50% of the financial support comes from state sources, 43% from local sources and 7% from the federal government. The state support for education comes from the state's general revenue funds (mainly from taxes), state school trust funds, lottery, and other funds that are appropriated to meet the needs of categorical programs and specific allocations.

Other state funds come from proceeds from licensing of motor vehicles and gross utility taxes which support capital outlay, racing commission funds, and other minor sources such as mobile home licensing.

Local support for education originates when the school boards levy the millage required for the local tax effort, which is determined by the state statutory process. The greatest source of funds are "Ad valorem" taxes, these are taxes levied on real estate or personal property. Additionally, voters may approve other tax levies such as maintenance bonds and operation-user fees. Federal funds to support education are administered by the Board of Education. These funds are provided to support federal mandates such as the National School Lunch Act, the Americans with Disabilities Act, and others.

From the appropriated funds, the district builds its budget. At this point, the budget becomes an important device for translating the educational plan into a financial plan. The budget is, in effect, the translation of prioritized educational needs into a financial plan, which is interpreted for the public in such a way that when it is formally adopted, it expresses the kind of educational program the community is willing to support financially and morally for a one-year period (Drake and Roe, 1994).

The funds or account groups are accounting entities with a self-balancing set of accounts that supports specific school activities to attain specific objectives. Therefore, funds or accounts can only be used for specified purposes. There are eight major funds or account groups: General Funds, Debt Services Funds, Capital Project Funds, Special Revenues Funds, Enterprise Funds, Internal Services Funds, Trust and Agency Funds, General Fixed Assets, and General-Long-Term Debt. Of all the funds, the General Fund is perhaps the most important to schools and school districts because it deals with the day-to-day operations of school.

A predetermined local formula allows expenditures from the General Fund to be used for the day-to-day operations of schools. Additionally, the school may have an Activity account and a School Internal account, which are managed by the principal. The Activity account is derived from class fees, athletic contests and events, plays, yearly photos, and other special programs. While the proceeds belong to the school, they must be used for students' learning benefits such as award ribbons, trophies, and the like. These proceeds must be identified and accounted for in the same manner as any other funds of the school.

The school internal account usually originates from vending machine sales in the teacher's lounge and from related faculty activities and must be used to benefit faculty and staff. Again, these proceeds must be identified and accounted for in the same manner as any other funds or accounts of the school.

The management of resources at a school is a very difficult task. Principals are required to maintain budgets, identify funds from external sources, manage staffs of usually twenty to one hundred teachers (in addition to support personnel), and keep track of material resources, such as office supplies, building materials, and instructional resources. How can a principal effectively do all this? First, every district has specific policies and procedures. The first thing a new principal should do is learn those procedures. Second, where a principal has discretion, attention should be given to the school's mission and vision. When resources are not directed at meeting the vision and mission of a school, those important elements are not cultivated or attended to. Third, a principal can get the assistance of school personnel, parents, and other interested parties. Often, when schools have site-based management committees, those groups can represent various school needs that are affected by resource allocation.

After taking all those issues into account, as resources are actually allocated, various procedures should be followed to record transactions. For example, as staff are hired, principals can demonstrate alignment between the desired qualifications, the actual qualifications of the hired individual, the district policies, and the school's mission and vision. Doing such recording helps prevent concerns about decisions that are made.

The management of human, material, and financial resources requires careful documentation, clear policies, and effective communication. Resources of all types carry emotional and personal weight with school community members. Principals who forget about the political elements of running a school often find themselves having to repair relationships. Proactive principals, however, consider all the political elements that might surface as decisions are made.

Skill 5.3 Demonstrating knowledge of how to use needs assessment, various types of data, and management skills and practices (e.g., time management, group process, consensus building, conflict resolution, team building) to make resource decisions and promote achievement of the school and district vision

**TX Skill 8.3 Acquire, allocate, and manage human, material, and financial resources according to district policies and campus priorities.**

**Skill 8.3 Acquire, allocate, and manage human, material, and financial resources according to district policies and campus priorities.**

ORELA 5.3

The management of resources at a school is a very difficult task. Principals are required to maintain budgets, but also find funds from external sources, manage staffs of usually twenty to one hundred teachers (in addition to support personnel), and keep track of material resources, such as office supplies, building materials, and instructional resources. How can a principal effectively do all this? E~~First, e~~very district has specific policies and procedures. The first thing a new principal should do is learn those procedures. ~~Second, w~~Where a principal has discretion, attention should be given to the school's mission and vision. When resources are not directed at meeting the vision and mission of a school, those important elements are not cultivated or attended to. ~~Third, a~~A principal can get the assistance of school personnel, parents, and other interested parties. Often, when schools have site based management committees, those groups can represent various school needs that are affected by resource allocation.

After taking all those issues into account, as resources are actually allocated, various procedures should be followed to keep track how things are done. For example, as staff are hired, principals can demonstrate alignment between the desired qualifications, the actual qualifications of the hired individual, the district policies, and the school's mission and vision. Doing such things helps to prevent concerns about decisions that are made.

The management of human, material, and financial resources requires careful documentation, clear policies, and effective communication. Resources of all types carry emotional and personal weight with school community members. Principals who forget about the political elements of running a school often find themselves having to repair relationships. Proactive principals, however, consider all the political elements that might surface as decisions are made.

Skill 5.4 Demonstrating knowledge of how to develop and implement plans for promoting and supporting communication and collaboration among personnel, and between district personnel and community members

**PRAXIS Admin Skill 5.5 Creating and maintaining a positive affective environment, such as existing school cultures' communication flow, and informal leadership**

**Skill 5.5 Creating and maintaining a positive affective environment, such as existing school cultures' communication flow, and informal leadership**

**ORELA 5.4**

All parents have deeply personal reasons to support the school's efforts: they want their children to do well in school. Some parents will have strong opinions about how the principal should run a school; if they were star students they will want the principal to replicate their school experiences. But many parents have memories of their own schooling that are less than positive, and these memories hamper their involvement in the school. Principals must constantly communicate the school's vision so that parents understand what the school is trying to accomplish. Uninformed parents and community members can derail the best improvement efforts.

Educating parents and the community about the school's programs, goals, and outcomes is a key responsibility of the school principal, but such communication will be different for every school building and school community. The parents are as diverse as the student population; they also have varying degrees of understanding and prior knowledge about the educational process. Communicating in a variety of ways will enable you to reach your goals of parent and community involvement. Fullan writes about the power of three- teachers, parents, and students working together. Parental support is an unleashed force that must be tapped for effective school improvement.

Successful principals share leadership, they reach out to their parents and community, and they work hard to expand the professional capacity of the teachers to develop a coherent professional community. Effective leaders create energy, bring harmony, forge consensus, set high standards, and develop a "try this" future-orientation. They are forever hopeful and cause everyone in the school's community to share this hope.

Skill 5.5 Demonstrating knowledge of how to use a variety of technological tools to facilitate communication

TX Skill 4.5 Facilitate the use of technology, telecommunications, and information systems to enrich the campus curriculum

**Skill 4.5 Facilitate the use of technology, telecommunications, and information systems to enrich the campus curriculum.**

**ORELA 5.5**

Technology, especially computer technology, is viewed by many as an advantage in achieving a school's stated learning objectives. The use of technology in achieving ~~the~~ learning objectives is not as widespread as it should be. Few of America's 2.8 million teachers are using technology in their teaching (Hancock, 1993; Office of Technology, 1995). What accounts for slow pace of technology's diffusion and integration into teachers' practice? Kearsley and Lynch (1994) concluded that teachers and administrators are not prepared to advance and manage technology in schools.

One can attribute the lack of adoption of technology in the teaching and learning environment to a number of causes, which~~. These causes~~ can be characterized under the headings of organizational factors and individual factors (Hope, 1997). Organizationally, integration of technology is hampered by a lack of specific plans. Incorporating technology into the teaching and learning process requires access to the technology that is to be used in the teaching environment. Because technology is expensive, teachers often do not have access to the technology. As well, teachers need training in the use of technology. The lack of effective training opportunities for teachers to visualize the capabilities of technology impedes its use in classrooms.

Leadership is an important ingredient in adopting technology and using it in the teaching and learning process. Without leadership from principals, teachers are often reluctant to introduce new methodology into the learning process. Because teachers are familiar with the processes and methodologies of earlier generations of teaching, and technology is a recent phenomenon, many do not have the background for using technology in the classroom. Teachers resist integrating technology into the teaching and learning process when they have not been exposed to the advantages technology affords beyond the methodologies they presently use.

The thrust to use technology in the learning environment is not likely to abate in the near future. So, for school administrators, it is important to recognize the capabilities of technology and the advantages it brings to the classroom, as well as becoming an advocate for using technology. A major responsibility falls on the school leader to model technology use and to also provide access and training for teachers to use technology.

The use of technology in schools by teachers and students is contingent ~~up~~on an understanding of the capabilities of various technologies~~y~~ and an ability to integrate these capabilities into the curriculum framework of a school. The application of technology to curriculum goals and objectives is an important function of school leadership. Involving students in learning sequences that utilize technology provides a new and motivating context to learning. Proponents of technology assert a significant role for technology in the teaching and learning process. They view technology as an ingredient with potential to transform the relationship between students and teachers and the dynamics that take place in the classroom. Computer technology offers teachers and students a constructivist learning environment, an~~. That is,~~ opportunity~~ exists~~ for students to engage in hands-on learning.

The placement of computers in individual~~ teacher's~~ classrooms offers the most benefit. This placement maximizes both teacher and student access to technology. Computers can be used in schools for achieving a number of instructional objectives:~~. They can be used for~~ remediation, drill and practice, and to simulate real world activities. Effective teaching utilizing technology is available. Understanding the appropriate application of technology to specific curriculum and learning objects is a key administrative skill. Knowing which applications of technology advance student learning is necessary.

Educational technology ~~evidences itself~~surfaces in many forms in schools. By far, however, the computer and various software applications predominate as the technology of choice in the teaching and learning environment. In an era of constructivist thinking in classrooms, where students take charge of their own learning, computer technology is perceived as an advantage to students' working independently, learning to think critically, and using computer technology as a productivity tool.

Technology should support the curriculum of a school, and~~. It~~ should be used~~tilized~~ to obtain the objectives and outcomes desired by school leaders, the community, and ultimately the nation. Determining how best to incorporate computer technology into the curriculum ~~should be~~is a time-consuming ~~a~~ process ~~that not a little time is spent on~~. In fact, the appropriate design and integration of computer technology into a schools curriculum is a major undertaking.

~~Integrating computers into school curriculum takes on the character of more than the aspect of fun.~~ Computers can only be significant in the teaching and learning process when the advantages and applications are carefully thought out and implemented. T~~here are t~~raditional uses of computers in classrooms, ~~lik~~such as~~e~~ drill and practice, games, and remediation under-use~~. However,~~ the capabilities of computers and software applications, which can be ~~make it~~ a versatile teaching tool with infinite potential ~~beyond traditional computer use~~. Computer technology can be used to support students in analysis, creative thinking, and problem solving. Specifically, information management, writing, and mathematical concepts can all be taught ~~to students~~ using the computer.

Video also has a powerful potential for education (Maurer & Davidson, 1998). Video formats have the potential for being the most creative educational applications developed thus far (Picciano, 1998). Moving images have an advantage over still visuals in the teaching and learning process. Video can be used in the learning environment for both affective and cognitive learning. Video technology comes in a variety of formats. ~~These are~~ DVD, videodisc, videocassette, (U-matic and VHS), videocassette (8 millimeter), and compact discs~~. DVD, videodisc and videotape~~ are common media being used in the instructional process ~~in schools~~ today.

Each of these formats presents advantages and disadvantages in the instructional environment. Video technology can be used to analyze human interactions, mastery of skills through repeated observations, and the shaping of attitudes (Heinich, Molenda, Russell, & Smaldino, 1996). However, in the classroom, it can promote in-active learning. Teachers need to ensure that their use of video technology in the classroom is appropriated for deep learning~~, only~~.

Skill 5.6 Demonstrating knowledge of principles and procedures for initiating, managing, and evaluating change in educational environments

**TX Skill 7.5 Encourage and facilitate positive change, enlist support for change, and overcome obstacles to change.**

**Skill 7.5 Encourage and facilitate positive change, enlist support for change, and overcome obstacles to change.**

ORELA 5.6

Change is always easier to talk about than it is to accomplish. Yet change must be a consistent element of organizational vitality. Determining when to change and what to change in the organizational milieu presents difficulties for a leader. People resist change for a variety of reasons. Perhaps the most prominent barrier to change is the threat it poses to individual roles and the perceived security individuals have in an organization. Human beings resist change almost instinctively. Regardless of the way a certain task is being performed, individuals engaged in performing it are familiar with the details and comfortable using the existing format. Change is viewed as disruptive because members of an organization have devoted energy and resources to accomplishing certain tasks in prescribed ways. To alter the methodology used to accomplish the tasks engenders threat to competency—given a new way of doing it, individuals are not sure they can accomplish the task. Change entails the prospect of discarding the old way of doing something for a new way of doing a task. So much has been invested in the old way that it is very difficult to acknowledge another method. As well, there is a legitimacy of the old versus the unknown qualities of the new.

Change entertained for the organization should be well thought through. Several points are illustrative and serve as advice for a change agent. The change that is to be introduced should not be done abruptly, but rather mentioned and discussed over a period of time preceding its intended implementation. Considerable support for the change should be marshaled so that it has sufficient sustaining forces in the organization. Details regarding the specific goals that are to be addressed by the change are important.

Furthermore, when change is top-down, or driven entirely be a school principal, for example, change is viewed as a threat. Successful change comes from allowing teachers in a school to be central in the decision-making and implementation process. While studies of decentralized decision making (or site-based management) are mixed on the impact of involving teachers in management decisions, in general principle, top-down imposed change causes more anxiety and is less effective at actually effecting real and significant change.

Doll (1996) discusses the process of change from three different perspectives. First, change is viewed as technical; that is, an innovation can be designed carefully and implemented into an organization with needed technical assistance.

Second, change is political, meaning that there are special interests of individuals at work in the planning of change. The third is cultural. Each planned change has potential for disturbing or altering the cultural context.

The Northwest Regional Educational Laboratory used a modified version of the five classic steps in the change process in a plan called the *research utilizing problem solving process.* Those steps are (a) identifying a need for change, (b) diagnosing the situation in which change is to take place, (c) considering alternative courses of action, (d) testing the feasibility of a plan for change, and (e) adoption, diffusion, and adaptation of successful change effort. This plan presents one approach to the change process that concentrates primarily on the initiation phase of a change process.

The change process is further complicated when there is no (or very little) existing support structure for the change or innovation to be introduced in the organization. Generally, a different kind of support system is necessary to maintain the change once it is introduced. It is important for a school leader to be aware and to begin to develop a support system for change in the school environment. Teachers are the ones expected to implement innovations and sustain change in the school. For change to be successful, attention must be given to them and their emotional and professional needs regarding change. ~~If~~ Neglecting teachers' emotional and professional needs ~~are neglected, the~~creates difficulty with change or innovation~~ will quite likely create difficulty~~. Change occurs best in a non-punitive,low-pressure~~-less~~, supportive environment. School leaders who foster change on this basis increase the likelihood of change becoming legitimized in the school.

Skill 5.7 Applying knowledge of principles and procedures for educational goal setting, data-driven decision making, and problem solving, and for involving constituents in aligning resources and priorities to promote the success of all students

**PRAXIS Skill 3.7 Applications of evaluation and research findings in the process of goal setting and change**

**Skill 3.7 Applications of evaluation and research findings in the process of goal setting and change**

ORELA 5.7

Goal setting is one way to bring about change in the instructional techniques used by teachers. It is also instrumental in school growth and improvement. At the beginning of each school year the whole staff should set at least three goals that are in line with the school mission statement or focus for the year.

Goals should be measurable, which means they should be specific. Applying the SMART method will ensure that the goals are achievable and can be evaluated.

The SMART method is:

- S – specific

- M - measurable
- A – achievable
- R – relevant
- T-time-framed

When goals are specific, it is easy to evaluate whether or not they have been achieved. The planning process should also identify resources the teachers need or will use to help achieve the goals.

At regular intervals throughout the year, the administrator should meet with each teacher to discuss the goals and how achievement is progressing. The administrator, through visitations to the classroom, will also be able to comment on what is happening and offer advice to the teacher on how to proceed.

**While some goals can be accomplished in one school year, some may need to be carried over to the following year.**

**COMPETENCY 6.0 Understand how to manage operational plans, procedures, and schedules at the school and district level to ensure a safe, effective, and healthy learning environment and promote achievement of educational goals**

Skill 6.1 Demonstrating knowledge of how to manage school and district operations effectively within the structure of Oregon public education rules, regulations, and laws and how to develop, implement, manage, and modify operational plans, procedures, and schedules to maximize student learning

PRAXIS Skill 4.4 Operational procedures at the school and district level; line staff relationships

**Skill 4.4 Operational procedures at the school and district level; line staff relationships**

ORELA 6.1

The administration of the school is responsible for the proper operation of the school. The office staff reports to the administrator and performs the duties outlined in their contracts. The administrator is also responsible for ensuring that the custodial staff keeps the school clean and up to health and fire-code standards.

The line of organization of any school district has the superintendent at the top. There is also a board of trustees or school board to whom the superintendent must report. Beneath the superintendent there is the district office staff, which consists of a deputy superintendent, the human resources director, the financial officer, and the various coordinators responsible for specific subjects. The principal of the school is next in line, followed by the vice-principal and then the staff.

Each of these individuals has a duty to perform and like there is a chain of command that has to be followed when reporting events or complaints. For example, instead of teachers reporting to the district office, they report to the principal, who in turn reports to the appropriate person at the district office.

**TX Skill 5.10 Analyze the implications of various factors (e.g., staffing patterns, class scheduling formats, school organizational structures, student discipline practices) for teaching and learning.**

**Skill 5.10 Analyze the implications of various factors (e.g., staffing patterns, class scheduling formats, school organizational structures, student discipline practices) for teaching and learning.**

**ORELA 6.1**

Many factors influence teaching and learning in schools. Often, it is hard for teachers to see the impact of various factors, as they are most familiar with what happens in their own classrooms once the close their doors. Yet, the entire structure of the school and school day sends many messages about values. Let us go through a variety of factors separately.

- **Staffing Patterns**: It should come as no surprise that who we have teaching our students makes a significant difference in how students learn. Of course, ~~with collective bargaining (union) regulating~~regulations limit how teachers are hired and fired, so many principals must learn to coexist with teachers who may not be very good. However, principals can find ways of minimizing the impact of poor teachers on the neediest students. Additionally, we all know that some teachers have specific strengths—and other teachers have entirely different strengths. It is useful to ensure that such teachers ~~are spread out~~assigned so that ~~as many~~ students ~~can~~ benefit from as many teachers' strengths as possible.

- **Class Schedule Formats**: Particularly at the secondary level, formats of schedules are critical to successful student learning. Many schools now see the value of block scheduling, a format that allows classes to meet for much longer periods of time on an alternating day schedule. Other schools have combined Social Studies with Language Arts or Math with Science in order to encourage cross-disciplinary studies. Some schools have students clustered in "houses" where all teachers rotate the same group of students. The purpose of this format is to allow teachers to discuss specific student issues. At the elementary level, class scheduling might permit students, for specific subjects, to be grouped homogonously. This allows teachers, in those subjects, to work more closely with specific student issues. Conversely, at other times, students can be grouped heterogeneously in order to provide a diverse climate among students.

- **School Organizational Structures**: ~~Typically, i~~In secondary schools, organizational structures typically refer to departments or grade-level configurations. In elementary schools, organizational structure is based on grade levels and non-core subjects. In both cases, organizational structures have a bearing on scheduling, physical location, and personnel. For example, secondary schools that have "houses" are typically better positioned to deal with student emotional issues. A student's teachers would have better access to one another—in a physical sense—to provide services and support. At the elementary level, an organizational structure that allows grade-level teachers to work in physical proximity to special needs' teachers is conducive to better collaboration on students learning requirements.

- **Student Discipline Practices**: From a student motivation perspective—as well as a building climate perspective—the ways in which a school handles discipline directly impact teaching and learning. H~~First, h~~igh expectations with reasonable consequences must be clear to all students and teachers. F~~Second, f~~air procedures must be followed. Teachers need to know that if they send students out of their classrooms that they must follow procedures, as well. The attitude at a school is more productive, though, when the emphasis is taken off of rules and consequences, and instead put on fairness, kindness, and other positive elements. When everyone sees that the school values equity more than it values rule-following, ~~for example,~~ people in the school will be more inclined to consider the value of the rules when they must be considered.

Skill 6.2 Applying knowledge of procedures and practices (e.g., record keeping, repair and maintenance, custodial services), and legal requirements (e.g., Oregon fire safety code, OSHA regulations) for ensuring the safe, efficient, and effective operation of school facilities

**FELE SKILL 1.10 Knowledge of managing the learning environment standard as related to facilities management**

**School Safety and Security**

School leaders are charged with providing students a safe, efficient, comfortable school building. While school districts and funding levels play significant parts in the aesthetics of a school building, basic safety and comfort issues are the responsibility of a school's administrative team. Various strategies can be put into place in order to promote satisfactory levels of building safety and efficiency.

A principal—or designee, such as an assistant principal—should be responsible on a daily basis to make rounds on a campus in order to verify a checklist of items. Such items might include visiting restrooms to ensure that everything is working properly and that students have clean, well operating facilities to use. A checklist might also include examining blacktop in the athletic areas to ensure that students would be safe running or playing on outside surfaces.

The school building must be in an operable condition. Any broken item that could pose a safety risk should be dealt with. Furniture that gets in the way of door areas must be moved. All doors should be completely operable and able to be opened quickly in an emergency. Windows should be able to be opened. Air conditioners, heaters, gas systems, plumbing, and electricity should all be able to be turned off easily and quickly if the need arises. This last point is a particular concern for many schools. If a specific custodian knows how to complete all those procedures, other individuals also need to learn how to operate such equipment in the case of that custodian's absence.

The principal must also advocate for building comforts at the district and community level. For example, while not all districts can afford air conditioning, principals can make needs clear to local taxpayers (with superintendent approval). While many school districts pay for utilities, school building leaders can examine utility usage for efficiency. Problems may be noted in terms of air drafts, heating duct problems, and plumbing.

Finally, school leaders should report problems that pose safety or privacy concerns to the district buildings manager. For example, if a bathroom stall door does not work properly, either a building level custodian must fix it, or if the building level resources are not available, a district support staff member should fix it. The same is true for issues of safety, such as a ceiling panel that is about to fall off in a classroom.

For information on assessing your school's risk during a crisis event see the website of the National Clearinghouse for Educational Facilities: http://www.ncef.org/pubs/mitigating_hazards.pdf.

Administrators must also be familiar with the Oregon Fire Safety Code, which can be accessed at http://www2.iccsafe.org/states/oregon/07_fire/fire07_frameset.htm.

Another important safety organization is the Occupational Safety & Health Administration (OSHA), which resides under the Department of Labor and was created through the Occupational Safety and Health Act of 1970. The administration is charged with protecting workers and makes such rules as requiring protective equipment be provided to employees where necessary and that employers eliminate dangerous chemicals such as asbestos. More information can be obtained at the OSHA website at www.osha.gov.

Skill 6.3 Demonstrating knowledge of how to develop and implement plans and procedures for ensuring student and staff safety and building security

TX Skill 9.1 Implement strategies that enable the school physical plant, equipment, and su

Tx Skill 9.2 Apply strategies for ensuring the safety of students and personnel and for add

**Skill 9.1 Implement strategies that enable the school physical plant, equipment, and support systems to operate safely, efficiently, and effectively.**

*ORELA 6.3*

School leaders are charged with providing students a safe, efficient, comfortable school building, conducive to rigorous academic learning. While school districts and funding levels ~~do~~ play significant parts in the aesthetics of a school building, basic safety and comfort issues are the responsibility of a school's administrative team. Various strategies can be put into place in order to promote satisfactory levels of building safety and efficiency.

A~~First, a~~ principal—or designee, such as an assistant principal—should be responsible on a daily basis to make rounds on a campus in order to verify a checklist of items. Such items might include visiting restrooms to ensure that everything is working properly and that students have clean, well operating facilities to use. A checklist might also include examining blacktop in the athletic areas to ensure that students would be safe running or playing on outside surfaces.

~~Another area a principal can be responsible for is in~~The principal must also advocate~~ing~~ for building comforts at the district and community level. For example, ~~While~~ while not all districts can afford air conditioning, principals can make needs clear to local taxpayers (with superintendent approval)~~, as one example~~.

While many school districts pay for utilities, school building leaders can examine utility usage for efficiency. Problems may be noted in terms of air drafts, heating duct problems, and plumbing.

Finally, school leaders should report ~~to the district buildings manager if certain~~ problems ~~exist~~ that pose safety or privacy concerns to the district buildings manager. For example, if a bathroom stall door does not work properly, either a building level custodian must fix it, or if the building level resources are not available, a district support staff member should fix it. The same is true for issues of safety, such as a ceiling panel that is about to fall off in a classroom.

## Skill 9.2 Apply strategies for ensuring the safety of students and personnel and for addressing emergencies and security concerns.

*ORELA 6.3*

Schools must be safe places for students to learn and for teachers to work. When emergencies occur, clear procedures must be in place to ensure that the school community responds in an orderly fashion. Details for planning and implementing safety plans are explained in the next section. ~~This section, however, will discuss specific strategies to ensure that safety is a priority in a school building.~~

T~~First, t~~he building must be in an operable condition. Any broken item that could pose a safety risk should be dealt with. Furniture that gets in the way of door areas must be moved. All doors should be completely operable and able to be opened quickly in an emergency. Windows should be able to be opened. Air conditioners, heaters, gas systems, plumbing, and electricity should all be able to be turned off easily and quickly if the need arises. This last point is a particular concern for many schools. ~~Often,~~If a specific custodian knows how to complete all those procedures, ~~. However, if that individual was not on campus at a particular time,~~ other individuals ~~would~~ also need to learn ~~know~~ how to operate such equipment in the case of that custodian's absence.

In planning for evacuation, routes should be drawn so that each hallway has the least amount of students walking through it possible, with no student having to walk too far. ~~In other words, usually, t~~The quickest route out of a building may clog a hallway, thereby making the route much slower. However, it would also be unwise to have a whole classroom full of students walk far around a particular hallway and still be in a potentially dangerous location. Often, fire departments or safety consultants can assist in designing solid, quality evaluation plans.

A lock-down plan ~~The~~is the opposite of an evacuation plan, and ~~would be a lock-down plan. A lock-down plan would~~ consists of various rules and procedures for getting or keeping all students in a secure location, such as a classroom. ~~The problem with a lock-down is often that~~Often communication suffers during a lock-down, ~~.~~so ~~M~~many schools ~~around the country are~~ now insist~~ing~~ that school personnel look at their email accounts as soon as a lock-down occurs, ~~as email is often a very~~to give the administration an efficient way to communicate to many people quickly.

In all, the best method of keeping students and staff safe is careful planning. ~~But, as we will see in the next section, i~~It is crucial that all school community members know those plans well.

Skill 6.4 Demonstrating an understanding of crisis planning and emergency management

Tx Skill 9.3 Develop and implement procedures for crisis planning and for responding to crises

**Skill 9.3 Develop and implement procedures for crisis planning and for responding to crises.**

*ORELA 6.4*

To ensure student and personnel safety, ~~a variety of~~various levels of planning must be implemented. P~~First, p~~lans must exist for ensuring safety in a variety of situations. Local natural disasters must be accounted for, as should plans for ensuring safety when, for example, the police are searching for a loose criminal in the surrounding neighborhood. Many schools may even have to consider safety plans for local terrorist attacks, particularly if the school is located near a busy or popular area.

Plans should include methods for getting students in a safe area, as well as communication among staff members and ~~communication~~ between administrative personnel and parents or media.

The next level of ensuring safety concerns communicating those plans to staff, parents, students, and the district. Fire drills, for example, do not command great attention from most staff and students, typically because most people have never experienced a fire in a large institution~~, such as a school~~. However, good administrators find creative ways to ensure that all staff members and students know the procedures. Clear directions~~, however,~~ should be posted all over a campus for clarification when events ~~do~~ occur. Directions and procedures should be mailed home to parents annually, as well.

When disasters or safety concerns ~~do~~ occur, school leaders must behave like flight attendants: c~~C~~alm and~~,~~ collected, but decisive and clear. People in the school community will ~~be more likely to~~ behave in a positive, productive manner ~~in a disaster~~during an emergency when the leadership gives clear instructions, is open and honest, and maintains a sense of peace ~~among decisive action~~while acting decisively.

After events that compromise safety, school leaders must do a few things. First, they must report all factors immediately to district administrators, local police, parents, students, and sometimes media. Second, they must sit down with other staff members and discuss the performance of the school community in responding to the crisis. From that discussion, the team can then make informed modifications to the plans. New plans, of course, must then be communicated to all stakeholders.

Skill 6.5 Demonstrating knowledge of strategies for developing a master schedule and for allocating and utilizing space to meet instructional and before/after-school program needs

A master schedule is used to allocate resources towards various educational activities. Schedule priorities are given first to core subject areas such as math, English, science, social studies, and reading. After these activities have been placed on the master schedule, programs of secondary importance are assigned to specific times and locations. Tertiary activities may include those programs that contribute to student development, but that do not directly impact upon key educational areas.

In addition to time considerations, space allocations must be clearly thought out and executed. Classrooms may be allotted according to subject areas, teacher assignments, or educational levels. For instance, in some schools, certain floors will be dedicated to freshmen and others to upper-classmen. The master schedule then, considers this predetermination when making space allocations. Other spaces are designated for multipurpose use and will float between permanently assigned tasks and open availability to be used on an as needed basis. Gymnasiums and cafeteria spaces are prime examples. In some cases schools are designed with one room serving as a cafeteria space during meal times, a gymnasium when required, and the theater/auditorium at times when plays and other performances are being held.

The final type of room assignments involves specialty areas such as computer labs and libraries. Unlike multipurpose spaces, these areas often cannot be adapted for various purposes. A computer lab must be monitored closely and the equipment contained therein is often too costly to justify allowing a multitude of activities to be held in this space. One strategy for reducing costs is to combine both the library and the computer lab into a media center or other single designation.

When adding activities to the master schedule, an administrator must ensure that he or she uses the fairest, most efficient, least controversial method to make assignments. It should be clear and well understood which assignments have priority and why. In some instances it is appropriate to make room assignments based on teacher seniority or subject area importance. Particular attention must be paid when making extracurricular assignments especially to student groups and organizations. Preferences should not be given to particular religious organizations or social clubs. Administrators must have a system to clearly communicate how space will be given and they must then adhere to this policy. In this way their integrity will not be compromised and negative repercussions can be avoided.

Skill 6.6 Demonstrating an understanding of procedures, practices, and legal requirements (e.g., federal and state regulations related to student transportation, immunizations, free and reduced meals) for managing auxiliary services (e.g., food, transportation, health services)

**TX Skill 9.4 Apply local, state, and federal laws and policies to support sound decision making related to school programs and operations (e.g., student services, food services, health services, transportation).**

**Skill 9.4 Apply local, state, and federal laws and policies to support sound decision making related to school programs and operations (e.g., student services, food services, health services, transportation).**

ORELA 6.6

Title VI, The Civil Rights Act of 1964 extends protection against discrimination on the basis of race, color, or national origins in any program or activity receiving federal financial assistance. *Clark v. Huntsville, Tyler v. Hot Springs*

Title VII, The Civil Rights Act of 1964 states that it is unlawful for an employer to discriminate against any individual with respect to compensation, terms, conditions, or privileges of employment because of an individual's race, color, religion, sex, or national origin. Some exceptions are noted in this statute. It does not apply to religious organizations that seek individuals of a particular religion to perform the work of that organization. Where suspect classifications (those classifications having no basis in rationality) represent bona fide occupational qualifications, they are permitted. Classifications based upon merit and seniority are also acceptable under this statute. *Ansonia BOE v. Philbrook*

Title IX, The Educational Amendments of 1972 states that no individual shall be excluded from participation in, be denied the benefits of, or be subjected to discrimination under any educational program or activity that receives or benefits from federal assistance on the basis of sex. This statute covers the areas of admission, education programs and activities, access to course offerings, counseling and the use of appraisal and counseling materials, marital or parental status and athletics. *Marshall v. Kirkland*

Section 504, The Rehabilitation Act of 1973 indicates that "No otherwise handicapped individual... will be excluded from the participation in, be denied the benefits of, or be subjected to discrimination under any program or activity receiving federal financial assistance solely because of his/her handicap. *School Board of Nassau Co v. Arline*

The Age Discrimination Act of 1967 states that it shall be unlawful for an employer to fail or refuse to hire or discharge any individual or otherwise discriminate against any individual with respect to his/her employment because of an individual's age. This statute does allow an employer or employment to consider age as a bone fide occupational qualification (bfoq). *Geller v. Markham*

The Family Rights and Privacy Act of 1964 (FERPA) [ Buckley Amendment] states that no funds will be made available under any applicable program to any state or local educational agency, any institution of higher education, any community college, any school, agency offering a preschool program, or any other educational institution which has a policy of denying parents of students the right to inspect and review any and all official records, files, and data directly related to their children. This includes material incorporated into the student's cumulative folder such as identifying data, academic work completed, level of achievement, attendance date, testing results, health data, family background information, teacher or counselor ratings and observations, and verified reports of serious or recurring behavior problems. Each educational organization must establish appropriate procedures for granting access requests within a reasonable period of time (not to exceed 45 days).

- Parents have an opportunity for a hearing to challenge the record's contents, to ensure the record's accuracy, and to provide corrected or rebuttal information.
- Educational organizations must require written consent of the parent in order to release identifying information to external individuals and organizations. (The state specifies exceptions.)
- All persons, agencies or organizations seeking access to a student's record must sign a written form that must be included in the student file.
- Students who are 18 years of age or attending a post-secondary educational institution acquire the right of consent formerly held by the parent. "Directory information" can be released without consent. Such information includes the following: student's name, address, telephone listing, date and place of birth, major field of study, participation in officially recognized activities and sports, weight and height of members of athletic teams, dates of attendance, degrees and awards of attendance, degrees and awards received, and the most recent educational agency or institution attended by the student.

The Individuals with Disabilities Education Act (IDEA) requires that states adopt policies that assure all children with disabilities receive a "free and appropriate public education." The statute requires that each student's unique needs are addressed through an "individualized educational plan (IEP) and that extensive procedural requirements are put into place. Requirements allow for the withholding of federal financial resources to states that fail to comply with the statute. *Honig v. Doe, Hendrick Hudson Board of Education v. Rowley*

The Equal Access Act of 1985 states that is will be unlawful for any public secondary school which receives federal financial assistance and which has a limited open forum to deny equal access or a fair opportunity to or discriminate against any students who wish to conduct a meeting within that limited open forum on the basis of the religious, political, philosophical, or other content of the speech at the meetings. A limited open forum exists whenever a school grants an opportunity for one or more non-curriculum-related student groups to meet on the school premises during non-instructional time. The criteria for a fair opportunity provide that

- the meeting is voluntary and student initiated;
- there is no sponsorship by the school, the government, or its agents or employees;

- school agents or employees are present at the meetings only in a non-participatory capacity;
- the meeting does not substantially interfere with the orderly conduct of educational activities within the school;
- non-school persons may not direct, conduct, control or regularly attend activities of student groups.

This statute ~~does~~ authorizes the school, its agents or employees to maintain order and discipline on the school premises, to protect the well-being of students and faculty, and to assure that the attendance of the students at the meeting is voluntary. *Board of Education of Westside Community Schools v. Mergens*

The federal constitutional amendments cited ~~above all~~ contain powerful clauses, and educators must be careful to ensure that a balance is struck between the individual's constitutional freedoms and the state's compelling interest (e.g. to provide an appropriate educational environment).

Court cases that arise out of the federal constitution and/or federal statutes come under the jurisdiction of the federal court system. As noted earlier, when school administrators, teachers and school employees act in their official capacities, they represent the state. This has significant implications for analyzing actions performed in the course of official duties that could breach the constitutional and statutory rights of students, parents, teachers, and staff members.

> The Congress of the United States and state legislatures have the authority to attack discrimination by passing statutes that codify constitutional intent and even surpass that intent as long as the statutes do not violate the equal protection rights of others. Congressional statutes provide broader equal opportunity rights and remedies by linking the observation of those rights to federal dollars, by prohibiting acts that are not covered by the Constitution, and by creating remedies that are not available under the Constitution. The evidentiary requirements to establish statutory discrimination are lower than those required for constitutional discrimination~~.~~ (Valente, 1994, p.336).

**COMPETENCY 7.0 Understand principles and practices of human resource management, including Oregon's educator licensure requirements, and their use in ensuring the placement of qualified staff in all positions and the provision of effective instruction to all students**

Skill 7.1 Demonstrating knowledge of the roles and responsibilities of staff

**FELE SKILL 2.3 Knowledge of human resource development standard as related to recruitment, selection, induction, and retention of staff**

**SKILL 2.3 Knowledge of human resource development standard as related to recruitment, selection, induction, and retention of staff**

ORELA 7.1

1. Given policies for teacher recruitment, selection, induction, professional development, and retention, determine compliance with Florida Statutes and No Child Left Behind legislation.

2. Given an out-of-field teacher report, identify various methods for acquiring Florida Teacher Certification (e.g., highly qualified teachers, critical shortage, special needs).

3. Given a sample of an interview, identify violations of federal and State laws that protect an applicant from job discrimination (e.g., AIDS, civil rights, Americans with Disability Act).

The educational leader in schools has a myriad of duties and tasks. The most time-consuming involves human resource management and development. Educational leaders must know and understand human relations since schools are labor intensive and use 80% to 90% of a school's budget. Over time, the personnel management roles of school administrators have expanded. Therefore, an understanding of the many aspects and importance of personnel management is essential in creating and maintaining a successful and efficient school organization.

The role of the principal in selecting instructional and non-instructional personnel is often considered the most important aspect of the position. It is through people that the principal is able to achieve the mission of the school; therefore he or she should lead the staff in a collegial environment. The administrator should convey that school personnel are of greatest importance and the principal should do all that is within his or her power to provide the best working conditions. Once they are empowered, the personnel will subsequently be empowered to do what is best for the students.

**Hiring Personnel**

In selecting instructional personnel, the principal has many responsibilities. Planning, recruitment, and selection are essential aspects of securing personnel. Planning requires the principal to look at the current staff and plan for future short-term and long-term personnel needs. Using site-based management, the principal involves current personnel in developing and revising the personnel plan for the school.

During this process, consideration must be given to current staff, students, parents, the community, school district, and state and federal rules and regulations. Planning must be comprehensive, take place well in advance of the need, and allow sufficient time to prepare papers and get approval through the district system. The principal must know the process used in the school district to select personnel, including how assignments are determined and the impact of the collective negotiation contract (if there is one in the district). The plan must also provide for emergencies such as unexpected promotions, illnesses, resignations, and terminations.

Once the plan is completed, recruitment can begin; this is a critical component of successful human resource management. First, the principal must understand the procedure in his or her district. Recruitment must occur early whether the principal has control of the entire process and uses a selection committee or whether the district does the recruiting and has to give approval to fill the positions. Second, the administrator must identify sources for qualified applicants with staff diversify factoring in to the hiring mix. College and university career offices, schools of education, and career fairs at the state and local levels are among popular recruitment options Dialogue with colleagues and current school staff also offer opportunities to recruit new employees

The selection process involves screening the paperwork, interviewing candidates and checking references. The selection committee must understand the confidential nature of applicant information and must be charged with maintaining the integrity of the process. Using a job-related matrix for the position, each applicant's papers are evaluated against the criteria. Unqualified applicants are removed from the candidate pool. Although certification in field is one of the most crucial factors to consider, the quality of the application is also judged for training competencies, job stability, comprehensiveness, grammar, and neatness.

Qualified applicants are then interviewed, the most time–consuming phase of personnel selection. After candidates are notified of the time and location for the interview, the committee determines questions to be asked and criteria to judge the responses. Each candidate for a position must be asked the same questions and judged by the same criteria. The committee then submits to the principal the names of the most qualified applicants, usually three to five individuals.

The principal reviews the work of the committee, interviews the potential employees, and conducts reference checks. Notification is sent to candidates informing them of their selection or non-selection. Another good strategy is to visit the person's current or most recent place of employment. Principals often contact the institutions that trained the potential employee to obtain professional judgments about the candidate. Retrieving fingerprint records ensures that known criminals are not employed. Last, the principal recommends to the superintendent the person who should be employed.

### Highly Qualified Teachers

Administrators are responsible for recruiting, selecting and inducting effective school personnel. The significance of this responsibility can be seen in the current national research that shows that of all high school graduates only about 72% enrolled as freshman. The drop-out rate for high school students is estimated to be around 20-30%. The cost of securing the best teachers is directly translated into high graduation rates and lowered drop-out rates for students who have demonstrated proficiency and knowledge acquisition during their high school career.

With *No Child Left Behind* and its emphasis on "highly qualified teachers," principals have to abide by state and federal laws regarding licensure/certification and degrees. For example, all secondary subject-area teachers must have a degree (or demonstrate extensive competency, usually through a very rigorous exam) in the subjects they will be teaching.

In Florida, all instructional personnel must be certified. This generally occurs by state testing after the potential teacher achieves the appropriate educational degrees. Specific information about certification for both in-state and out-of-state applicants can be found at http://www.fldoe.org/edcert/.

### Retention of Qualified Personnel

An effective compensation and reward system is required in any organization. A compensation program attracts, maintains, and motivates quality employees. It also creates incentives for continual growth, and maintains budgetary control in school districts. Merit pay, paid leave, child care, cost of living increases, salary schedules, extracurricular stipends, early retirement plans, tax-sheltered annuities, and medical plans are types of compensation and rewards. In addition, social security benefits, retirement plans, severance pay, transportation allowances and leaves of various types (sick, annual, sabbatical, religious, military, and professional) are included. Supply and demand often determine the package available to employees.

Many districts are currently experimenting with pay for performance plans, where bonuses are given to teachers who increase test scores. This has been highly controversial, because statistical models to determine teacher impact on student test scores is rather complicated and imprecise.

A good induction process is also crucial to successful hiring and retention. Newly hired employees receive assistance because they usually need more support than experienced individuals. The first part of orientation is to introduce the procedures, paperwork required, teaching and learning expectations, rules, and other aspects of the school culture. In some systems the district conducts the orientation, with the school providing additional orientation for those factors unique to the school. The socialization process is another critical facet, it can determine how well new personnel adapt and contribute to the teaching/learning community. The induction process typically ranges from 90 days to a full school year. The best approach lasts a year and pairs a neophyte teacher with a mentor who teaches the same grade level and subjects.

Skill 7.2 Applying knowledge of fair and equitable practices and procedures for recruiting, hiring, assigning, retaining, evaluating, disciplining, and dismissing staff, including state and federal legal requirements

FELE SKILL 2.6 Knowledge of human resource development standard as related to processes and procedures for discipline, dismissal, and nonrenewal of school employees

**SKILL 2.6 Knowledge of human resource development standard as related to processes and procedures for discipline, dismissal, and nonrenewal of school employees**

**ORELA 7.2**

1. Given a recommendation to terminate an employee's contract, identify the school site administrator's responsibilities regarding termination as required in Florida Statutes (e.g., union contract, professional service contract, annual contract, continuing contract).

2. Given case studies with accompanying documentation, identify and apply the Standard of Just Cause for any adverse employment decision as required by Florida Statutes (e.g., dismissal, suspension, demotion, reinstatement).

The Florida statute *F.S. 231 Personnel* spells out the qualifications, selection processes, certification processes, the operation of the Education Standards Commission and the Education Practices Commission, leave policies, and contractual and termination procedures relating to school personnel. Reviewing this law in detail is necessary for a principal to adequately manage disciplinary issues under his or her purview.

Termination is one of the most difficult tasks that a school principal must perform. The guiding principle question should and must be: Is this teacher permanently harming children because of incompetence or marginal teaching and learning outcomes? There are only a few of these teachers for whom the answer would be yes; however, these few individuals can consume a high percentage of a principal's time. Thus, the principal must follow clear guidelines, maintain a careful record, and provide due process to the teacher.

First, the principal must identify the teachers who need support and notify them in a timely manner. Next, they should be offered assistance; the Employee's Assistance Program is one resource. The teachers can be counseled into other positions if they cannot become high-quality instructors. If the issues require punitive action, the teacher must be notified of charges in writing, adequate time must be given for the teacher to prepare a rebuttal. The teacher must be permitted counsel of his or her choice. During an impartial hearing, the teacher must be able to examine any evidence. When a decision is made based on the evidence, a transcript of the hearing must be given to the teacher. Lastly, he or she is allowed an appeal if there is a decision to terminate him or her or if there is a severe loss to the teacher.

Skill 7.3 Demonstrating an understanding of benefits of and procedures for recruiting and retaining diverse staff

Recruiting and retaining a diverse staff should be a priority for all administrators. When the term diversity is used, many people think of cultural or racial differences; however, diversity also includes differences in perspective, educational training, and thought processes. A school is greatly aided when it contains staff members who will expose each other to different ideas and unique ways of thinking. In order to establish and nurture a diverse staff, administrators must first recruit individuals who would bring diversity to the team.

One strategy for achieving this goal is to engage in recruitment efforts at myriad locations. For instance a school district should schedule recruitment fairs at major universities, small colleges, Historically Black Colleges and Universities, Hispanic-serving institutions, schools with large Native American populations, and institutions known for training candidates in nontraditional, yet highly effective ways. By starting out with a diverse pool of candidates, the administration is more likely to hire individuals who differ racially, culturally, and educationally.

Once diverse individuals are on the staff, it is just as important to retain their services and make sure that the entire team is able to work cohesively. The benefits of different perspectives can quickly become challenges if the administration is not prepared to overcome obstacles. It is not unusual for individuals to clash over culturally and personally accepted practices. It is up to the administration to foster an environment in which everyone can bring their perspectives without being put down or without being condescending.

Providing opportunities for all cultures and perspectives to be valued and celebrated also allows staff members to embrace being part of a diverse team. As with many challenging efforts, success requires the administration to internalize the value of diversity. This buying should lead to action, which should lead to a systematic process. This in turn leads to staff embracing each other's uniqueness. Rather than focusing on their differences, the staff enjoys working together and continues doing so because of their shared focus on educating children.

Skill 7.4 Applying knowledge of the collective bargaining process, including district policies and state and federal laws related to collective bargaining (e.g., Oregon's Public Employees Collective Bargaining Act)

**FELE SKILL 2.7 Knowledge of human resource development standard as related to collective bargaining agreements**

**SKILL 2.7 Knowledge of human resource development standard as related to collective bargaining agreements**

ORELA 7.4

1. Given a collective bargaining agreement, identify the role of the administrator in managing the contract per Florida Statutes (e.g., grievances, school policies, enforcement, and punitive actions related to all classifications of school personnel).

Collective bargaining is the process of negotiating a contract between the management of a school district and the teachers' union, which represents the teachers within a district. Although monetary matters comprise the majority of issues in most collective bargaining sessions, other facets of working conditions (such as job duties, hours on campus, etc.) are negotiated, as well.
A principal may serve on the school district's management team during a collective negotiation. The negotiation process is usually lengthy, involves multi-year contracts, team determination, unit recognition, planning and preparation, agreement and implementation, strategies to reach agreement, and counterproposals. While collective bargaining has typically been viewed as a divisive process, progressive unions and sensitive school districts have found that working together can be more beneficial to both sides.

Skill 7.5 Applying knowledge of policies and procedures related to human resource administration, including relevant state and federal laws and regulations (e.g., FMLA, ADA, COBRA)

Human resource management is a crucial part of an administrator's job. School of leaders must both manage employees and ensure compliance with federal, state, and local regulations. To achieve this goal, it is important that the administrator state of breasts of changes and additions to policies and that he or she is ready to adapt to update its standards. Although it is difficult to provide an exhaustive list of federal and state laws
relating to human resource management, several key regulations can be presented.

<u>FAMILY AND MEDICAL LEAVE ACT – FMLA</u>

Governed by the US Department of Labor, the Family and Medical Leave Act (FMLA) provides protection for employees who are facing serious health challenge or who must care for family members who have such health challenges. The act provides details concerning what consists of a serious health challenge, requirements for employees to be covered by the FMLA, and how the federal government protects employees from employers who abuse or don't comply with this policy.

Basic Leave Entitlement
FMLA requires covered employers to provide up to 12 weeks of unpaid, job-protected leave to eligible employees for the following reasons:
• For incapacity due to pregnancy, prenatal medical care or child birth;
• To care for the employee's child after birth, or placement for adoption or foster care;
• To care for the employee's spouse, son or daughter, or parent, who has a serious health condition; or
• For a serious health condition that

The Americans with Disabilities Act - ADA

The Americans with Disabilities Act (ADA) prohibits discrimination against people with disabilities. According to the federal government, compliance with ADA regulations involved more than simply making physical changes. In order to fully comply with the requirements agencies must assess their programs, services, and activities. They must shore practices do not automatically preclude individuals with disabilities from participating. For instance if animals are typically not permitted in certain facilities, policies must be adapted to allow for guide dogs.

An excerpt from the Department of Justice states the following:
While the ADA has five separate titles, Title II is the section specifically applicable to "public entities" (state and local governments) and the programs, services, and activities they deliver. The Department of Justice ("DOJ" or the "Department"), through its Civil Rights Division, is the key agency responsible for

enforcing Title II and for coordinating other federal agencies' enforcement activities under Title II.

In addition, the Department has the ability to enforce the employment provisions of Title I of the ADA as they pertain to state and local government employees. DOJ is the only federal entity with the authority to initiate ADA litigation against state and local governments for employment violations under Title I of the ADA and for all violations under Title II of the ADA.

More information on ADA regulations can be obtained on the following federal website: http://www.ada.gov/pcatoolkit/chap1toolkit.htm

Consolidated Omnibus Budget Reconciliation Act of 1985 - COBRA
Under the Consolidated Omnibus Budget Reconciliation Act of 1985 (COBRA) you and your dependents may be eligible to continue medical and/or dental coverage for a period of up to 18 months at your expense. You will receive information about the COBRA program by mail to your home address from BenefitHelp Solutions. You will have 45 days from the date your coverage ends to enroll in the COBRA coverage. You will be required to pay the premiums plus an additional two percent administrative fee during the months you are eligible for the continued coverage.

Skill 7.6 Applying knowledge of Oregon educator licensure and assignment rules to ensure that qualified staff are placed in all positions

**Skill 3.8 Instructional staff assessment, including conferencing, observation, data collection, and documentation of performance**

Appraisal of personnel is a significant part of a principal's responsibility; they must be able to hire and assign staff to appropriate positions. This will result in the greatest, most productive environment in which education can proceed and where students can thrive. Most districts establish district-wide criteria for hiring and promotional decisions. These guidelines are usually developed through a diverse committee of school and community representatives and provide principals with objective and reliable methods of hiring and appraising staff.

Once appropriate staff are hired, evaluations must be conducted on a regular basis. For many teacher evaluations, states require performance-based assessments; therefore, the principal must tie teacher performance to student learning. If the principal needs to acquire additional information on the development and implementation of the appraisal process, he or she can contact district or state officials, university professors, professional organizations, or consultants.

In an effort to support teacher success, the state or district may provide assistance to new and experienced teachers new to teaching in the state. The assistance of a peer teacher and a variety of induction activities enable teachers to receive assistance without the implied threat of evaluation. This open system allows these teachers to seek help when it is needed.

When the evaluation process is conducted properly, teachers grow professionally and students benefit from increasingly effective instruction. Teachers should set professional-development goals based on weak areas and should receive recognition for areas of strength. The processes for gathering the data used to rate teachers should also be published and discussed. Most often, there are formal, planned classroom observations, as well as informal walk-throughs and other informal methods for viewing a teacher's work.

Teacher performance ratings should be directly tied to student achievement, so student achievement data should be included in determining appraisal scores. The driving motto should be that teaching has not happened unless students have learned! Teachers should be given clear feedback about whether their performance is adequately satisfying the criteria of the appraisal instrument. Delivering this feedback to the teacher in a face-to-face conference allows the appraiser to establish a dialogue with the teacher about instructional practices. Very few professionals change simply because someone talks to them, this includes teachers. To change behavior, administrators must change the thinking behind the behavior. This can be achieved by asking questions that cause teachers to reflect on their own practices.

As a principal, your goal is to improve your staff so that student achievement will be optimized. You will encounter underperforming teachers who are in need of assistance. With these individuals, agree on two or three improvement goals and concentrate on making progress in these areas before moving on to other areas of need. Document the improvement plan andany progress, or lack of progress, toward the selected goals. Poorly trained teachers need to observe excellent role models, so allow release time for observations in other classrooms. Conferencing with the mentee after the observation will assist them in applying what they observed in their own classroom. When a teacher is working through an improvement plan, the principal should make more frequent visits to the classroom and look for signs of improvement. Document every visit and intervention. Ineffective teachers can improve with a principal's support, training, and mentoring.

The appraisal process is also a way to provide recognition for outstanding teachers. When a teacher's performance is highly rated, this provides encouragement to continue instructional practices that benefit students. Appraisal systems allow for the structured feedback that teachers need to improve instruction and grow professionally.

**Competency 8.0** Understand principles and practices of fiscal and material resource management and their use in promoting the achievement of educational goals.

Skill 8.1 Demonstrating knowledge of how to use planning and problem-solving skills to allocate fiscal, human, and material resources effectively, legally, equitably, and in ways that focus on teaching and learning for all students

**TX Skill 5.9 Analyze instructional needs and allocate resources effectively and equitably.**

**Skill 5.9 Analyze instructional needs and allocate resources effectively and equitably.**

**ORELA 8.1**

Many principals do not have control over entire personnel budgets (e.g., usually, district human resource offices control personnel issues at school sites), but schools often do have discretion over many resources, including materials, additional funding, and support services. In an age of accountability, funding for student achievement~~, accountability~~ must also be in place~~ for the use of funds~~. For a principal to make sense of the instructional needs at a school, various analyses must be done. First, by looking at student achievement, principals can see which groups of students require more resources. When referring to resources, the term equity is often used. This term may imply that all students should get the same resources—or same level of monetary allocations. The current thinking, though, is that in order to reach certain standards, different students will require different resources. Therefore, when leaders think about allocating resources effectively and equitably, it is helpful to consider the term adequacy. In other words, leaders can ask the question: What is adequate in providing each student what he/she needs to reach standards at high levels?

Another way to analyze instructional needs is to examine how money is allocated to various parts of a campus and to ~~reflect on~~determine which areas need ~~resources~~ a reallocated ~~so~~of funds to support ~~that~~ student achievement ~~is the first priority~~. Of course, when doing this, principals face great scrutiny from stakeholders who~~that~~ are negatively affected by shifts in allocations. Principals are more successful in this work when they enlist the support of a variety of stakeholders.

Finally, it is critical that principals make their practices public—to faculty, to parents, to the district, and to the community. Of course, small monetary issues are outside the interest of most stakeholders;~~,~~ however, the information should be available—and even discussed—as school funds are derived from taxpayers. Furthermore, when monetary decisions are public, support for decisions are much more easily acquired.

Skill 8.2 Applying knowledge of how to seek new resources to facilitate learning

**Georgia Skill 3.6 Secures the financial and human resources necessary to promote the educational vision**

**Skill 3.6 Secures the financial and human resources necessary to promote the educational vision**

ORELA 8.2

The administration of a school is responsible for ensuring that their building has the necessary resources to execute the educational vision and goals. Typically, schools receive a budget based on the number of students in attendance. Since preliminary budgets are prepared at the end of the school year for the next, the enrollment is a projected estimate of the number of students that will be in attendance in September.

From the total budget amount, the administration has to ensure that enough monies are available to pay the human resource expenses including teaching and clerical staff. When this is determined, the remainder of the money has to be budgeted to allow for new resources, textbooks, general supplies, pupil transportation and other expenses necessary for the operation of the school.

All monies spent must have the approval of the administration. The same thing applies to any monies raised through fundraising. When checks are written they should have two signatures, that of the principal or vice-principal and the secretary. The principal is responsible for ensuring that the secretary reports all expenditures to the financial officer at the school district level and that the supporting documents are in place for audit purposes.

Reports about the budget should be made known to the parent council. In cases where a deficit exists in one school year, the administration has to ensure that this is made up the following year, through cutbacks, if necessary. Careful records are necessary, both in hard copy and on the computer, so that everything can be scrutinized in the event of any problems that arise.

When money is paid to the school, either through fund raising, donations or fees, the secretary must issue receipts. This leaves a paper trail for all monies coming into the school.

Skill 8.3 Demonstrating knowledge of school finance in Oregon, including relevant laws and regulations (e.g., state and local revenue sources, capital and operational funding, school funding formula, federal funding)

http://www.ode.state.or.us/services/ssf/finance/estwarrants/2008-pbam-manual.pdf

Various local, state, and federal revenue sources finance schools in Oregon. The 1000-level revenue sources, those provided locally, are the greatest source of funds for schools. In this category are Ad Valorem taxes levied by the District on real property. Funds also come from taxes on construction, tuition paid on adult, continuing, and summer-school education. Transportation Fees, School lunch funds, and extra-curricular activities contribute to the coffers. Revenue from Intermediate Sources are categorized as 2000-level. State support is listed in the 3000-level categories and includes unrestricted funds such as school lunch funding and restricted funds such as those for drivers' education programs. Federal support, listed as 4000-level, also comes in the form of restricted and unrestricted funds. Other sources of income are categorized in the 5000-level and includes bond proceeds, mortgage receipts, and lease purchase receipts.

Skill 8.4 Analyzing the effects of school finance on the equitable distribution of educational opportunities within and between districts

**FELE SKILL 1.8 Knowledge of managing the learning environment standard as related to funding of Florida schools**

**SKILL 1.8 Knowledge of managing the learning environment standard as related to funding of Florida schools**

ORELA 8.4

1. Given an FTE report, identify, interpret, and apply each formula factor used in computing the Florida Education Finance Program allocation.

2. Given a school budget, identify funding categories available to a school beyond the Florida Education Finance Program allocation.

3. Given a school budget, identify or apply the processes of planning, developing, implementing, and evaluating a budget.

The *Program Budgeting and Accounting Manual* guides financial activities for public schools in the state of Oregon. The manual conforms with Generally Accepted Accounting Principles (GAAP), an industry-wide set of guidelines for financial accounting and reporting. Guided by Oregon Budget Law (ORS 294), districts are required to prepare and present their budgets on an annual basis. Therefore, each school administrator must be well versed in the financial operation of his or her school in order to submit the required reports on an ongoing and summative basis.

## Background Information on School Funding

Every state has its own funding formula to allocate general distribution of funds to local school districts. This formula can be complex because of the efforts of state legislatures to provide uniformity of support. While some public school programs are fully funded by the state, others may rely on flat grants, foundation programs, or a variety of tax-base-equalization programs.

Florida uses the foundation program where the state defines the level of funding for basic education. The state and the school district in partnership provide the funds required for the educational programs. Unlike the flat grant model, where the state alone provides per pupil funding, in the foundation program both the state and the districts act in partnership to determine the required level of local participation.

Major sources of support for public education come from revenues generated from taxes. Property tax at the local level, sales tax at the state level, and income tax at the federal level constitute primary sources of revenues for education. Legal provisions for funding public education come from the constitution. The lack of clear language and specificity of public school funding results in school funding litigations, which historically have led to major school finance reforms. Legislative enactment, regulations, decrees, or rulings are outgrowths of school finance litigations. These reforms originated from the basic values and beliefs of the citizens and leaders at the national, state, and local levels.

Early litigation of school finance alleged that the methods of financing education at the state level violated the equal protection for certain classes of people under the constitution. Allegations were also made that the reliance on local revenues to support a large portion of the total public school budget was unfair because of the disparity in property tax wealth among the school systems. There are four landmark court cases that built on each other to produce significant school financing reform.

In *McInnis v. Shapiro -1969*, the plaintiffs contended that the Illinois method of financing public education was inequitable because it permitted a wide variation in expenditures per student. This method of financing did not apportion funds according to the educational need of students. The court rejected the plaintiff's contention and stated that the controversy was unjustifiable because it lacked judicially manageable standards. The court further stated that equal expenditures per student were inappropriate as a standard. The court was ill-prepared to provide advice on an plan to equitably finance public schools because it lacked specific understanding of cost-effectiveness.

*Serrano v. Priest -1971* emerged after the precedence set by the previous case. In this situation, the plaintiffs contended that the California system of school finance allowed substantial disparities between the various districts in the amount of revenues available for education. They further contended that this method denied equal protection of the laws under the constitution of the United States and the constitution of California and that this system required some parents to pay taxes at a higher rate than taxpayers in many other districts in order to provide the same or lesser educational opportunities for their children. In this landmark decision, the court contended that education is a constitutionally protected fundamental interest and that wealth was a suspect classification. The court established the Standard of Fiscal Neutrality as a measurement to determine whether or not a school finance program was constitutional. Under this standard, the quality of the child's education could not be based on the wealth of the local school district, but on the wealth of the state as a whole.

In *Rose v. The Council of Better Education -1989*, the plaintiffs contended that the system of financing schools by the Kentucky General Assembly was inadequate because it placed too much emphasis on local school board resources which result in inadequacies and inequalities throughout the state. This resulted in an inefficient system of common school education, which violated the state constitution. The court ruled in favor of the plaintiffs and appointed a committee to review relevant data, provide additional analysis, consult with financial experts, and propose remedies to correct the deficiencies in the common school financing system.

Another landmark case in school finance is *San Antonio Independent School District v. Rodriguez - 1973*. The plaintiffs contended that the dual system of public school financing in Texas violated the equal protection clause of the Constitution of the United States and Texas. The initial ruling in 1971 held the state financing system of Texas unconstitutional under the equal Protection clause of the Fourteen Amendments. An appeal of this decision reversed the ruling because of unanswered questions concerning the constitution of Texas. But in the second ruling, the court found substantial disparities among the districts' school expenditures, which were largely attributed to the differences in the amounts of the dollars collected through property taxes. The court concluded that the dual system of public school finance in Texas indeed violated the equal protection clause.

Overall, the courts have found that education is both a public and a private good because it enhances the individual as it brings important benefits to society. At an individual level, education provides the ability to enjoy a higher standard of living by earning more money and living a better quality of life. Society benefits because the individual makes a contribution to the economy. Education supports the production of a skilled workforce for the efficient functioning of a society that is stimulated by economic growth and development.

## Educational Budgeting

A main educational function of the state governor is to formulate budgetary recommendations for the legislature. In Florida, the governor depends on his or her appointed advisors and the elected Commissioner of Education as the main support in policy discussions and recommendations. While the governor has many powers, the position holds some limitations in personnel decisions. All Commissioners, the Secretary of State, and the Comptroller make up the Cabinet. The Cabinet approves State Board Rules. The Governor and each member of the Cabinet has only one vote. In Florida, the governor does not appoint the Commissioner of Education; the citizens do so through the electoral process. The governor also has veto power which serves to discourage the state legislators from enacting laws considered detrimental to education.

The process of financing schools is a yearly one. It is continuously reviewed to identify strengths and weaknesses so that meaningful and deliberate planning can take place to meet the needs of students. School administration has evolved into an inclusive and cooperative endeavor. The structure endorses a participatory model to include not only administrators and teachers, but also parents, business partners, and other interested citizens in the community.

Therefore, the planning process must be ongoing and systematic to allow time for the development of unity of purpose, methodology, and desirable outcome. At both the district and school-building levels, planning must be continuous and methodologies and applications may overlap. Planning follows a very logical sequence to accomplish organizational goals. It begins with setting goals, which includes articulating the mission of the organization and clarifying specific goals to be attained. It also means setting long and short-term plans of action that including general projections and details to carry out the actions deemed necessary. The evaluation process provides feedback for improvement and the process is repeated.

School financial management requires specific budgetary techniques for appropriate fiscal accountability. There are three commonly used techniques.

*Incremental budgeting* begins with the budget for the current term and examines each line item against expected revenues. By addressing expenditures by items and categories, there is a failure to observe the impact of the budget as a whole on the goals of the organization and the needs of children.It also hinders creativity and change.

*Zero-based budgeting* is another planning technique that produces similar outcomes as the incremental budgeting approach. It focuses on the current budgetary cycle and begins with zero dollars in all accounts to then justify the continuation of a program, activities, or expenditure.

In contrast, the *Planning, Programming, Budgetary, and Evaluation System* (PPBES) integrates long-range planning, the resources provided through funded sources are used to achieve institutional goals on the basis of annual fund allocations (Drake and Roe, 1994). This process requires the periodic collection and analysis of data to inform the decisions to be made about programs and to project needs to be met. The evaluation component that is built into the process not only assesses the effectiveness of the goal, but it also measures the level of goal attainment over specific periods of time.

## Funding Education in Florida

Early in the history of our nation, education became a local and state responsibility. The responsibility is granted to the legislature of each state through plenary power, which enables the enactment of laws it considers appropriate and desirable for education. Under this premise, the Florida legislature enacted the FEFP (Florida Education Finance Program) in 1973 to equalize the educational opportunities for every child in the state. Florida Statute section 236.012 defines its purpose as follows:

> "To guarantee to each child in the state of Florida public educational system the availability of programs and services appropriate to his educational needs which are substantially equal to those available to any similar student notwithstanding geographic differences and varying local economic factors."

Until the early 1970s, previous formulas for public school funding were generally based on a school system's wealth, which took a ratio of school taxable property and allocated it equally to each child in the system. This resulted in either wealthy school systems or poor school systems. The higher the taxable property, the wealthier the school system became and conversely, the lower the taxable property, the poorer the school system became. To equalize the available resources to all children in Florida, the FEFP recognizes in its formula, the following components:

- varying program cost factors to account for district cost differentials
- differences in per student cost for equivalent educational programs due to scarcity and dispersion of student population
- varying local property tax bases

Each year the Florida Legislature determines the minimum efforts of taxation on district property tax roils, as well as the program cost factors, to determine the base funding for each student. For participation in the state allocation of funds, each school board must levy the millage set for its required local efforts. Each district's share is determined by certification of the property tax valuations by the Department of Revenue and the Commissioner of Education. Assessment ratios are used to equalize the effects of the FEFP on differing levels of property appraisals in each county. Millage rates are also adjusted to ensure that the required local rates do not exceed 90% of the district total FEFP entitlement. Ultimately, the state's appropriation is used to fund the difference between the amount raised for each student through the required local millage, times the property tax roll, plus the established base student allocation.

Since a key feature of the FEFP is based upon student participation in a particular educational program, the varying program cost factors set by the legislature are essential to the formula when determining base funding. To better understand the formula, here are definitions to key terms:

*FTE*: A full-time equivalent student

*Weighted FTE*: An FTE multiplied by a program cost factor

*Base student allocation*: a fixed amount determined each year by the legislature

*District cost differential*: The Commissioner of Education annually averages each district's Florida Price Level Index for the last three years and applies the prices of salary on district operating cost to reduce its impact on the district.

The base student funding is calculated by multiplying the full-time equivalent student (FTE) by the program cost factor, which gives the weighted FTE. The weighted FTE is then multiplied by the base student allocation and the district cost differential to produce the base student funding as seen below.

FTE x program cost factor = weighted FTE

Weighted FTE x base student allocation x district cost differential = BASE STUDENT FUNDING

Other FEFP factors authorized by the Legislature are added to adjust and finalize the distribution of funds to each school district. These adjustments include declining enrollment supplements, sparsity supplements, safe school allocations, remediation reduction incentives, discretionary tax equalizations, and hold-harmless and disparity-compression adjustments.

Apart from the FEFP formula, each district may levy discretionary millage, which is a level of additional discretionary taxes. This amount is authorized by the legislature with a proportion of it equalized with dollars from the state for categorical funds including instructional materials, student transportation, instructional technology, and food services. Another categorical fund outside the FEFP formula is preschool funding which comes from lottery proceeds. All of these considerations make the FEFP a model program for the equalization of educational opportunities for all children in the state of Florida. To participate in the FEFP, every district must provide annual evidence of its efforts to maintain an adequate school program throughout the district and must meet at least the following requirements:

1. Maintain adequate and accurate records including a system of internal accounts for individual schools, and file with the Department of Education correct and proper forms, on or before the date due, each annual or periodic report which is required by state Board of Education Rules.

2. Operate all schools for a term of 180 actual teaching days or the equivalent on an hourly basis. Upon written application, the State Board may prescribe procedures for altering this requirement.

3. Provide written contracts for all instructional personnel and require not less than 196 days of service for all members of the instructional staff.

4. Expend funds for salaries in accordance with a salary schedule or schedules adopted by the School Board in accordance with the provisions of the laws and rules of the State Board.

5. Observe all requirements of the State Board relating to the preparation, adoption, and execution of budgets for the district school system.

6. Levy the required local effort millage rate on the taxable value for school purposes of the district. In addition, collect fees for adult education courses.

7. Maintain an ongoing systematic evaluation of the educational program

needs of the district and develop a comprehensive annual and long-term plan.

## Sources of Funding

There are three major sources of school funding for the school districts in the State of Florida. Approximately 50% of the financial support comes from state sources, 42% from local sources, and 7% from the federal government. The state support for education comes from the state's general revenue funds (mainly from taxes), state school trust fund, Florida Lottery, and other funds that are appropriated to meet the needs of categorical programs and specific allocations. Other state funds come from proceeds from licensing of motor vehicles, gross utility taxes (which support capital outlay), racing commission funds, and other minor sources such as mobile home licensing.

Local support for education originates when the school boards levy the millage required for the local tax effort, which is determined by the state statutory process. The greatest source of funds is "Ad valorem" taxes (taxes levied on real estate or personal property). Additionally, voters may approve other tax levies such as maintenance bonds and operation-user fees. Federal funds to support education are administered by the Board of Education. These funds are provided to support federal mandates such as the National School Lunch Act, the Americans with Disabilities Act, and others.

Proceeds from the lottery are used to finance both district discretionary lottery funds and preschool projects. Education's share of the revenue is 38% which goes into the Educational Enhancement Trust Fund and is distributed at a rate of 70% for public schools, 15% for community colleges, and 15% for universities.

Future resources for education are planned through student enrollment forecasts. This is a joint effort between the Florida Department of Education, the Governor's Office, the Legislature, and the school districts. The forecast input is essential for the FEFP appropriation, primarily because it is used to compute district allocations and make actual payments until the student membership can be determined through certified surveys. This process is defined by Florida Statute section 216.136(4).

## Local Budgeting and Accounting

From the appropriated funds, the district builds its budget. At this point, the budget becomes an important device for translating the educational plan into a financial plan. The budget is, in effect, the translation of prioritized educational needs into a financial plan. Ideally, the budget is interpreted for the public in such a way that, upon adoption, it expresses the kind of educational program the community is willing to support financially and morally for a one-year period.

The budget must be managed through a financial system of accounting. In the state of Florida this system is predetermined for the school districts and is managed through the Financial and Program Cost Accounting and Reporting for Florida Schools, also known as The Red Book. It deals only with revenues and expenditures. Revenues are categorized by sources. Sources of revenues can be federal, state, or local. Expenditures on the other hand, are categorized by dimensions, which include funds or account groups, objects, functions, facilities, projects, and reporting.

The funds or account groups are accounting entities with a self-balancing set of accounts that supports specific school activities to attain specific objectives. Therefore, funds or accounts can only be used for specified purposes. There are eight major funds or account groups: General Funds, Debt Services Funds, Capital Project Funds, Special Revenues Funds, Enterprise Funds, Internal Services Funds, Trust and Agency Funds, General Fixed Assets, and General-Long-Term Debt. Of all the funds, the General Fund is perhaps the most important to schools and school districts because it deals with the day-to-day operations of school.

The budget of the district is generally comprised of the account groups or funds established by the Red Book. Since many of the accounts held by the district are not appropriate to the school operation, the school account differs from that of the district. For example, most districts are responsible for salaries and benefits, utilities and services, therefore, these accounts are not included in the school-based budget.

A predetermined local formula allows expenditures from the General Fund to be used for the day-to-day operations of schools. Additionally, the school may have an Activity account and a School Internal account. The Activity account is derived from class fees, athletic contests and events, plays, yearly photos, and other special programs. While the proceeds belong to the school, they must be used for students' learning benefits such as award ribbons, trophies, and the like. These proceeds must be identified and accounted for in the same manner as any other funds of the school.

The School Internal account usually originates from vending machine sales in the teacher's lounge and from related faculty activities and must be used to benefit faculty and staff. Again, these proceeds must be identified and accounted for in the same manner as any other funds or accounts of the school.

**For more information about FTE go to the Miami Dade County Public Schools website:**

http://attendanceservices.dadeschools.net/fte.asp. It includes a helpful PowerPoint presentation with samples from an actual FTE report entitled 2007-2008 Elementary Training FTE Self-Review PowerPoint Presentation

Skill 8.5 Applying knowledge of procedures for developing and managing balanced district, school, and department budgets, including relevant laws and regulations (e.g., Oregon School Budget Law), and for involving constituents in budgeting processes

TX **Skill 8.1 Apply procedures for effective budget planning and management.**

TX Skill 8.2 ............................Work collaboratively with stakeholders to develop campus budgets

**Skill 8.1 Apply procedures for effective budget planning and management.**

ORELA 8.5

School administrators must be knowledgeable in basic accounting principles to provide appropriate fiscal management for the economic and efficient operation of the school. Accounting is the process used by administrators to record, present, summarize, and interpret accurate records of the financial data collected by the school through its daily operation. These basic accounting principles lead practicing administrators to the recognition of revenues and expenditures for the pre-established accounts of the school.

General principles of school cost accounting require using~~the utilization of~~ an accrual basis for accounting rather than a cash basis. This means that the financial transactions of the school must be recorded as revenues or expenditures at the time the transaction occurs and there should never be cash exchanged for goods or services. ~~This generally accepted principle is called the accrual basis of accounting. In this process,~~With accrual basis accounting, revenues earned at the time of the transaction become assets, and expenditures become liabilities, regardless of when the cash receipt or reimbursement occurs;~~. In this system of accounting~~ assets are inventory, investments, accounts receivable, building and fixed equipment, furniture, motor vehicles,~~etc.~~ while liabilities are salaries, benefits, accounts payable, construction contracts~~, etc~~. Unlike private, for-profit enterprises ~~for profit~~ where there is owners' equity, schools are owned by the taxpayers, and~~. Therefore,~~ balances are known as fund equity, which include reserves, retained earnings, contributed capital, and other fund equity.

Schools must adhere to specific rules governing their internal funds as prescribed by State Board Rules. All school organizations must be accountable for receipts and expenditures of funds obtained from the public. Additionally, sound business practices are expected for all financial transactions of the school. For example, in an effort to raise money to benefit programs of the school, fund-raising activities should not conflict with the programs administered by the school board.

All purchases from internal funds must be authorized by the principal or designee and district's pre-approved, serially numbered receipt forms must be used to record any cash received and to record the accounting transaction. Each school must have a bank checking account and each monthly statement must be reconciled as soon as it is received. Each account should have two authorized check signers, one being the principal. The principal should be never pre-sign checks or purchase orders, under any circumstances. Monthly written financial reports must be made for the purpose of school decision-making, and annual reports must be made for the district's annual financial statement.

The sponsors of classes, clubs, or department student activities (such as athletic events, musical, and the like) are responsible for providing the financial documents and records to the principal or designee. They must deposit money ~~The collection~~ received ~~must be deposited~~ in the school internal fund in the ~~respective~~appropriate classified account (athletics, music, art, Latin Club, and others). All disbursements by the dub or organization must be made by check from internal funds. A financial report must be filed with the principal's office at the close of each fundraising activity.

Records and documents of school financial transactions used for its internal fund and accounts must be examined periodically through the auditing process. This auditing process, whether internal or external, provides an adequate safeguard to preserve the property of the public school system. This process secures evidence of propriety of completed transactions; it determines whether all transactions have been recorded, whether these transactions have been accurately recorded in the appropriate accounts, and whether the statements have been drawn from the accounts.

Good auditing reviews are the result of excellent accounting practices. Drake and Roe (1994) define the accounting cycle as continuous and inclusive of the processes of documenting, analyzing, recording, and summarizing financial information. Documenting includes recording all financial transactions including the authority or initiator of the transaction, ensuring that the debt incurred is within the limit of allotment, that every financial transaction is identified with a unit or fund, and that each fund is restrictive and limited in use. The process of analyzing requires that each transaction is analyzed and classified into debits and credits, and that each debit and credit is referenced to a specific account under the affected fund.

**The school operation must** always be ~~very~~ conscious of its fiscal control to avoid over-expenditure and maintain a positive balance in each of its accounts. Therefore, an encumbrance system must be used to charge each purchase order, contract, or salary to an appropriation. Once paid, these transactions are canceled and ceased to be an encumbrance as soon as the liability is recorded.

Future resources for education are planned through student enrollment forecasts.
From the appropriated funds, the district builds its budget. At this point, the budget becomes an important device for translating the educational plan into a financial plan. The budget is, in effect, the translation of prioritized educational needs into a financial plan, which is interpreted for the public in such a way that when it is formally adopted, it expresses the kind of educational program the community is willing to support financially and morally for a one-year period (Drake and Roe, 1994).

The budget must be managed through a financial system of accounting. Revenues are categorized by sources. Sources of revenues can be either federal, state or local. Expenditures on the other hand, are categorized by dimensions which include funds or account groups, objects, functions, facility, project, and reporting.

The funds or account groups are accounting entities with a self-balancing set of accounts that supports specific school activities to attain specific objectives. Therefore, funds or accounts can only be used for specified purposes.

At the school level the district allots a certain number of dollars based on a predetermined local formula to allow expenditures from the General Fund related to the day-to-day operation of the school. Additionally, the school may have an Activity account and a School Internal account. The Activity account is derived from class fees, athletic contests and events, plays, yearly photos, and other special programs. While the proceeds belong to the school, they must be used for students' learning benefits such as award ribbons, trophies, and the like. These proceeds must be identified and accounted in the same manner as any other funds of the school.

The school internal account usually originates from vending machine sales in the teacher's lounge and from related faculty activities and must be used to benefit faculty and staff. Again, these proceeds must be identified and accounted for in the same manner as any other funds or accounts of the school.

### Skill 8.2 Work collaboratively with stakeholders to develop campus budgets.

ORELA 8.5

The process for working collaboratively with stakeholders to create a campus budget is very similar to the school improvement process. The school principal should first gather information from as many stakeholders as possible, including certified and non-certified staff, parents, students, and other community members. Once that data has been collected a school budget committee could be formed with representation from each of these groups.

The first goal of this committee should be to create a common vision. This vision should show a relationship between the school's budget and its school improvement goals.
Since all members of the committee may not be familiar with creating a school budget, it will be important to provide instruction for the members. Committee members should be provided with an explanation of the statutes that affect the school's budget. It may also be necessary to discuss the role of the stakeholders in the budget process. The school principal may wish to share proposed budget allocations, curriculum needs and plans, and new programs and district initiatives. At that point the principal should ask for input from the stakeholders and also present the data that was collected at the beginning of the process.

After the budget has been created, the committee may discuss ways to report expenditures throughout the school year. This may be done through monthly meetings or other communications, such as memos or emails.

The final step in the process is for the committee to present the proposed budget to the district for approval. If there are areas that are not approved, the committee should reconvene to make any necessary changes.

Skill 8.6 Demonstrating knowledge of procedures for communicating and reporting accurate financial information to a variety of audiences (e.g., school boards, community members)

**Georgia Skill 8.4 Reporting financial information annually to staff and the public in ways that clarify expenditures and assessment results**

**Skill 8.4 Reporting financial information annually to staff and the public in ways that clarify expenditures and assessment results**

ORELA 8.6

Financial expenditures require the signature and approval of the administrator and typically one other designee. Rather than making budgetary decisions based on whim or favoritism, the principal should always be guided by the campus improvement plan and his/her leadership team. For example, if funds are requested for an autism conference, but there are no school goals or student needs in this area, then this request should not be funded. Conversely, if the school goals include literacy development, then the principal should approve a request to purchase additional library books. Resources are always limited, and conflicts can occur when stakeholders are denied their requests for purchases.

The principal can minimize problems and maintain integrity by: involving the school leadership team in budgetary decisions, keeping the group focused on student achievement, and reminding everyone of the school vision.

After the allocation process has been determined, the principal must develop a system to accurately track all funds obtained and spent. To avoid serious consequences or charges of fund misappropriation, cash transactions must be handled very carefully. This can be facilitated by minimizing the use of cash. If this form of payment is unavoidable, district-supplied, serially-numbered receipt forms must be used to record any cash received as an accounting transaction. Additionally, each school must have a bank checking account and each monthly statement must be reconciled as soon as it is received.
Monthly written financial reports must be made for the purpose of school decision-making, and annual reports must be submitted for the district's annual financial statement. All these steps make it easier for the administrator to prepare annual reports for the district, the school staff, and the public. Though the format and content of the reports will differ for the different audiences, it is important that all stakeholders be valued and included in this crucial aspect of school operations.

Skill 8.7 Applying knowledge of district finance structures and models to ensure adequate and equitable resource allocation

Education in most states is primarily funded through property taxes at either the state or local levels. This is true for the state of Oregon as well. Funding based on property taxes automatically creates a disparity between districts where property values are high and those where they are low. Many states grapple with strategies to reduce this difference and in so doing, seek to educate all students equally. These issues fall under the heading of equity. Part and parcel with equity is the matter of access; which is a student's ability to obtain and benefit from resources that are necessary for an adequate education.

In 1990, Oregonians began addressing issues of adequacy, equity, and access by voting for Ballot Measure 5. While this substantially reduced property taxes levied at the local level, it was in 1991 that the state Legislature passed a new school equalization formula that increased state funding. During that year, 25% of state budget and lottery revenues were used for education. By 2005, the allocation had increased to 44% of these funds.

Currently, the K-12 School Equalization Formula is represented by the following chart presented by the Oregon Department of Education:

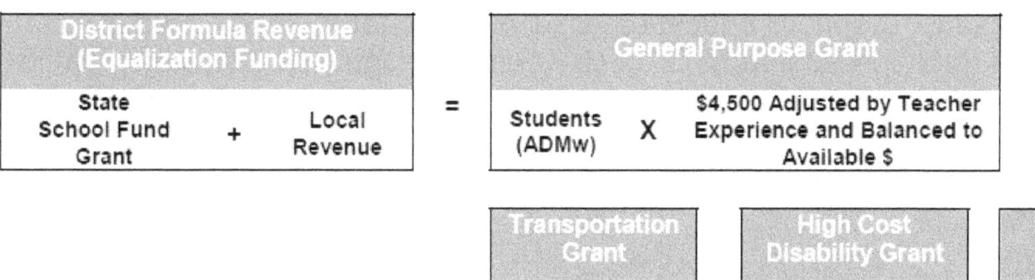


**The terms in the formula are defined by the state legislature and much of the language below is quoted directly from the legislative publication:**

### District Formula Revenue (Equalization Funding)

**State School Fund Grant** is State School Fund money available for distribution to school districts.
**Local Revenue** includes property taxes, County School Fund, Common School Fund and a few other sources. No changes were made to local revenue sources included in the formula.

**The General Purpose Grant** starts at a $4,500 target per weighted student. For purposes of the formula, "student" means weighted average daily membership (ADMw) extended. Weighting means counting a higher cost student as more than one. Extended means the higher of the current year or prior year ADMw.

**Teacher Experience Factor** increases or decreases the $4,500 per student target by $25 for each year the district average experience is more or less than the statewide average teacher experience.

### Transportation Grant

The transportation grant is a 70% to 90% reimbursement of approved student transportation costs. These costs are primarily school bus costs for transport between home and school and class field trips. Districts are ranked by costs per student. Districts ranked in the top 10% have 90% grants. Districts ranked in the next lower10% have 80% grants and the bottom 80% of districts have 70% grants.

### High Cost Disability Grant

**High Cost Disability Grant = Up to Sum of Costs above $30,000 per Disability Student**

A district's high cost disability grant is the sum of the approved disability costs for each special education student that exceeds $30,000 per year. The school district can add ESD special education costs incurred for the same student for the student's total special education cost. Keeping a high cost disability grant in the formula reduces the general purpose grant total by the same $12 million. Thus all districts share in the cost and those with high cost disabilities benefit when their high cost disability grant exceeds the reduction in their general purpose grant.

**Facility Grant**

**Facility Grant = Up to 8% of Construction Costs**

Districts with rapidly growing student populations typically have a greater need to equip new facilities compared to districts with stable or declining student populations. In the funding equalization formula, this is covered in the facility grant, which can be up to 8% of construction costs.
In 2005-07 this grant was not to exceed $17.5 million and is prorated down if eligible costs exceed $17.5 million. Beginning in 2007-09 the grant total cannot exceed $25 million and is prorated down if eligible costs exceed $25 million in a biennium.

More information can be obtained from the legislative document at http://www.ode.state.or.us/services/ssf/2005SchoolFinanceLegislation.pdf.

### Skill 6.6 Allocating and deploying financial and human resources to sustain the instructional program

The management of school resources is a very difficult task that includes maintaining budgets. Principals must secure funds from external sources, manage a staff between twenty and one hundred people, and keep track of material resources, such as office supplies, building materials, and instructional resources. Every district has specific policies and procedures for managing and allocating resources. Therefore, the first thing a new principal should do is learn those procedures. Second, attention should be given to the school's mission and vision. When resources are not directed at meeting the vision and mission of a school, those important elements are not cultivated or are ignored. Third, a principal should rally the assistance of school personnel, parents, and other interested parties. Often when schools have site-based management committees, these groups can represent various school needs that are affected by resource allocation.

After taking all these issues into account, various procedures should be followed to keep track of how resources are actually allocated. For example, as staff are hired, principals can demonstrate alignment between the desired qualifications, the actual qualifications of the hired individual, the district policies, and the school's mission and vision. Engaging in this process will help to prevent concerns about decisions that are made.

The management of human, material, and financial resources requires careful documentation, clear policies, and effective communication. Resources of all types carry emotional and personal weight with school community members. Principals who forget about the political elements of running a school often find themselves having to repair relationships. Proactive principals, however, consider all the political elements that might surface as decisions are made.

Allocating money for professional affiliation is often overlooked. Principals and teachers should belong to at least one association in their field. They can then access the literature that will provide updates on what is going on in that field. It is also advised that educators attend at least one gathering of their association. Getting away and talking to colleagues from other parts of the country help administrators and instructors avoid entrenchment. Listening to what is happening in the field is also useful. It is rare that an educator attends one of these conferences without making changes in the way his or her school or classroom is run. Therefore, school and district budgets must include financial resources to support and encourage all staff to engage in mandatory and optional professional development opportunities that create a "win-win" situation for educators and students.

Skill 8.8 Demonstrating knowledge of types of financial records, procedures for accurate record keeping and reporting, including legal requirements, and the use of current technologies for financial management and business procedures

Various types of financial records exist and administrators must be proficient in overseeing each type. The first group includes accounting documents such as monthly accounting statements and detailed transaction reports. Second are purchases of materials and services requisitions including purchase orders, invoices, travel documents, and vouchers. The third group of documents are loosely termed receiving documents because they track goods and services obtained by the school or district. Among these records are credit card receipts, packing slips, and delivery confirmations. Lastly, administrators must maintain payroll documents tracking employees, hours worked, salaries and other funds paid, benefits, and taxes.

In addition to executing and recording financial transactions, administrators must also report on these activities. The Oregon Department of Education groups financial reports as either internal or external. Internal reports include:

- Comparison of budgeted vs. actual revenues and expenditures;
- Cash flow projections;
- Building operation and maintenance costs;
- Expenditure accounts, showing activity during the last reporting period; and
- Comparison of current and prior year's revenues and expenditures.

Conversely, external reports are defined as those to be used by non-district users and may include:

- General financial/statistical summaries for use by legislators;
- Specific reports of certain revenues and expenditures by program, for use by the funding source(s); and
- Program cost reports.

Skill 8.9 Demonstrating knowledge of procedures and legal requirements associated with procurement, bidding, and vendor relationships

**TX Skill 8.4 Apply laws and policies to ensure sound financial management in relation to accounts, bidding, purchasing, and grants.**

**Skill 8.4 Apply laws and policies to ensure sound financial management in relation to accounts, bidding, purchasing, and grants.**

ORELA 8.9

The primary role of school administrators is improvement of student achievement, but they are also responsible for managing the campus finances. Administrators must understand their campus budget in relation to the district's budget allocation, as well as the rules and policies that regulate how schools may spend their funding. Because principals are not typically trained in accounting concepts, they often rely on bookkeepers or secretaries to maintain these records with little oversight. This lack of supervision can result in a loss of funds that can lead to loss of community trust and even an administrator's career.

So what does an administrator need to know about school finance? ~~First of all, u~~Understanding the politics involved in the process of funding schools should be a concern for school administrators. Every state has its own funding formula to allocate general distribution of funds to local districts to provide educational services to children. This formula is usually very complex because of the efforts of state legislatures to provide uniformity of support. In most states, the funding for education comes from a blending of federal, state and local revenues usually generated from taxes. ~~There are many instances of school funding litigations with~~ A~~a~~llegations that a system of funding based on taxes leads to disparity in property tax wealth among school systems have led to litigation. Federal and state mandates and policies have direct implications for school level implementation of programs to meet the needs of children, especially when the level of funding is incongruent with the requirements of the law. Unfunded mandates put an unnecessary burden on local districts and schools and have led to an increase in local fundraising for items necessary to carry on the business of the school. Helping legislators understand the financial implications of their programs or mandates at the district and campus level should be a priority for school administrators.

At the school level the district allots a certain number of dollars based on a predetermined local formula to allow expenditures from the General Fund related to the day-to-day operation of the school. Additionally, the school may have an Activity account and a School Internal account. The Activity account is derived from class fees, athletic contests and events, plays, yearly photos, and other special programs. While the proceeds belong to the school, they must be used for students' learning benefits such as award ribbons, trophies, and the like. These proceeds must be identified and accounted in the same manner as any other funds of the school. General accounting procedures are designed to meet three important school financial objectives: (1) to protect school staff from suspicion of theft, (2) to protect school assets, and (3) to fulfill the public's expectation that public funds will be spent responsibly. The use of school activity funds is "restricted" which means that the funds are not yours to lend, borrow, or spend in any way you like. You must follow the following principles:

- You may use the funds only for the purpose for which those funds have been raised.
- If funds have been raised by the entire student body they must be spent to benefit the entire student body.
- If students are old enough, students should have representation, with faculty supervision, in the management and spending of the funds raised by the student group.
- Activity funds should be spent on the students who were in school at the time they funds were raised.
- Fund-raising projects should not conflict or detract from the instructional program or put students in an unsafe situation. Many schools restrict students from door-to-door sales due to concerns for student safety.
- Activity funds should be managed with sound accounting procedures, including the use of receipts for all funds received.

Skill 8.10 Demonstrating knowledge of procedures for ensuring effective internal controls to safeguard building and district financial operations

**TX Skill 8.4 - end paragraph Apply laws and policies to ensure sound financial management in relation to accounts, bidding, purchasing, and grants.**

There are several types of internal controls that will assist a principal in overseeing the appropriate spending of campus funds. The policy of having principals approve all purchase orders will prevent misuse of funds. Having the principal review the monthly bank statements helps detect errors and incongruities in spending practices. If an error is found, the principal can follow up with the bank. Bookkeepers should be restricted to working only when an administrator is in the building. Relying on one person with little or no supervision is a recipe for trouble. If an administrator fails to place and maintain reasonable financial controls, then they may unknowingly become an ally to dishonest employees. A key control is an annual audit conducted by an independent financial company. This process is required by most states, including Oregon.

**Competency 9.0** Understand ethical guidelines and policies, laws, regulations, and judicial decisions affecting education in Oregon.

Skill 9.1 Applying knowledge of principles and guidelines for acting fairly, ethically, and with integrity in varied educational contexts

**PRAXIS Skill 3.9 Staff are treated fairly, equitably, and with dignity and respect**
TX **Skill 3.1 Model and promote the highest standard of conduct, ethical principles, and integrity in decision making, actions, and behaviors.**
**Skill 3.9 Staff are treated fairly, equitably, and with dignity and respect**
ORELA 9.1

All staff need and deserve to be treated with respect, whether they are part of the teaching staff or the custodial staff. Staff members need to know that the administration is there to help in any situation, will respect confidential information, and does not show favoritism. Aspects of dealing with members of the staff include:

- Interpersonal communication
- Retention of staff
- Civility
- Reward and recognition
- Developing teams
- Establishing trust
- Managing stressful situations
- Supporting staff in times of change

When a new administrator comes into a school, he or she has to develop a sense of trust with the staff. They need to know that the administrator will support them in cases of problem students or if problems arise with parents. Staff who do an exceptional job need to be recognized and this should be done publicly such as at staff meetings. The administrator should look for exemplary teaching or behavior in all staff, but at the same time rewards and recognition should not be handed out frivolously.

Team-building is important in schools but it will take time. The administrator has to make sure that the members of the team get along. Teams with members who cannot work together will not function effectively. An administrator also has to be able to manage stressful situations without panicking or becoming distraught. This will let the teachers know they have a leader on whom they can depend. At the same time, the administration has to support the school district in bringing in policies and programs with which teachers may not agree. Therefore there will be times when teachers will be forced to change. The administrator has to realize that change is not easy and that teachers should be coached to take small steps leading to change.

**Skill 3.1 Model and promote the highest standard of conduct, ethical principles, and integrity in decision making, actions, and behaviors.**

**ORELA 9.1**

Principals are leaders. Their behavior, stated communication, and implied communication have a tremendous impact on those with whom they work. Others often follow the lead of the principal. If a principal is calm in difficult situations, the students, parents, staff, and faculty will usually assume this position; the reverse is also true.

A principal who resolves conflict in a systematic, fair manner promotes this kind of behavior within the school. The means ~~by which~~ a principal uses to share~~s~~ information and reach~~es~~ decisions are closely observed and followed.

The principal who shows partiality or insists that his or her position is the only one will not obtain meaningful input from those with whom he or she is working. ~~A result of this kind of management behavior is that~~In this type of environment people will say what they expect the principal to say, say nothing, or agree with the principal's views. The result is that the best results are not achieved since the best collective thinking of the learning community is not a part of the planning, implementation, and evaluation of the work of the school. If the principal appears to close or open up discussion, others in the environment will respond accordingly. A strong principal realizes that there are times when decisions must be made and makes them in a timely fashion. For example, if a person enters the campus with a gun, the principal must take action to provide safety for everyone. If teachers have conflict, the principal must find means to resolve the problem before it becomes a major deterrent to achievement of organizational goals.

Confidence in public education has eroded over the past several decades. Numerous private, parochial, charter, and other types of schools have emerged during this period. Concomitant with these~~is~~ ~~movement and resulting from public dissatisfaction with public schools~~shifts is an increased attention to providing vouchers for~~to~~ parents to~~for~~ use in selecting a school~~s~~ of choice for their children. The perceptions of the public relative to students, faculty, staff, administration, and the total school are significant in the community's attitude about a school.

Management of a school requires a clear understanding of knowledge about the importance of this public perception, as well as techniques to handle successes and problems.

Schools handle accomplishment in a variety of ways. Brochures, speaking engagements, and student presentations are successful avenues. Cultivating a friendly relationship with all local media benefits a school since the good news is reported and the bad news is often given in a positive manner. Establishing ~~A~~a school committee ~~is considered one outstanding way~~ to handle public relations and to work with the media under the leadership of the principal is often effective. The public relations committee could also prepare press releases to share the "good news" about the school.

Many people say that perception is reality. The importance of perceptions by a school's community can never be overlooked. If the school is to be perceived in a positive light, it must control negative information about the students, staff, faculty, administration, and total school. The best control strategy is to remove those situations that create **negativity**. Additionally, the physical appearance of the school's building and grounds, as well as the behavior and achievements of its students, contribute to the school's image. The principal is required to manage these aspects of the school.

Skill 9.2 Applying knowledge of Oregon State Ethics Laws for Public Officials and Ethical Educator Standards

Chapter 244 of the Oregon Blue Book contains the laws and regulations governing ethics requirements for public officials in the state of Oregon. Also known as ORS 244, the law can be found at http://www.leg.state.or.us/ors/244.html. These regulations are intended to maintain the public trust by requiring public officials to refrain from activities that compromise the integrity of their positions. Sections of the law address issues such as the definitions of terms used within the law, limits on gifts that can be accepted by officials, parameters of lobbying efforts, and nepotism.

It is important for educational leaders to be aware of the specific guidelines contained in this law. Knowing and abiding by the requirements will safeguard the administrator's integrity and maintain the public trust. In addition, it will ensure that a school official does not engage in actions that could jeopardize his or her position. One of the most common ethical issues is a conflict of interest of which ORS 244 lists two types, actual and potential. The first type, actual conflict of interest is defined in 244.020(1) as the effect an action WOULD or WILL have; in contrast, the second type, potential conflict of interest, is defined in ORS 244.020(14) as the effect an action COULD have. They state that conflict of interest occurs whenever a public official makes an action, decision, or recommendation in his or her official capacity that results in a financial gain or loss by the official, his or her relative, his or her business, or the business of a relative. Again, in one case, the gain or loss WOULD or WILL occur and in the other, the gain or loss COULD occur.

Section 244.050 lists the individuals required to file a verified statement of economic interest with the Oregon Government Ethics Commission. Specific deadlines and guidelines are also provided for this requirement. Public officials not listed is required to file this statement whenever there is a conflict of interest. an official is required to file a “statement of This section of the book also contains information on forms

Skill 9.3 Demonstrating knowledge of the content of Oregon's adopted standards for administrator licensure

See all sections contained in this guide book

Skill 9.4 Demonstrating knowledge of legal principles and practices for promoting equity in schools and school districts

See Skill 2.7 and Skill 5.2

Skill 9.5 Applying knowledge of local, state, and federal policies, laws, and regulations related to school administration (e.g., open meetings laws, liability, reporting requirements) and student and staff rights, protections, and responsibilities (e.g., due process, free speech, sexual harassment)

PRAXIS **Skill 4.13 Due process procedures for students and staff**
PRAXIS **Skill 4.14 Judicial and legislative provisions for students with disabilities, privacy act, affirmative action, sex discrimination, freedom of information, and civil rights**
**Skill 4.13 Due process procedures for students and staff**
ORELA 9.5

When students misbehave in school or break the school rules, administrators must follow due process. The first course of action is to interview the student and try to determine the reasons for the behavior. If the behavior is minor in nature, the principal may decide to give the student after-school detention with parental notification.

In-school suspensions are also quite common, under this method the student is not permitted to have contact with his or her peers during the day or part of the day in certain cases. If the misbehavior is of a major nature, the student is likely to receive an in-school suspension for the first offense. The parents and the school board should be notified in writing. Schools have their own rules for how many in-school suspensions must occur before the student is suspended from school for a specified period of time.

The type of punishment handed out to students also depends on the age and grade level. For middle school and high school students, suspensions of up to 15 days are possible after the second or third violation. In high schools, some actions may actually be illegal and the law enforcement agency has to be involved. Any parent who does not agree with the suspension or punishment meted out has the right to grieve the situation. This is done by meeting with the administration and the teachers involved. If this meeting does not resolve the situation, then a further meeting may be required with the superintendent.

The Due Process Clause of the Constitution of the United Sates indicates that no state can deprive any person of life, liberty, or property without due process of law. Liberty and property have been broadly defined to refer to a wide range of substantive rights. For example, educators' contracts provide them with a property interest and expectation of employment for the terms of the contract. Tenure provides an expectation of future employment and so endows the individual who has tenure with a property interest. Liberty interest has been defined to encompass a wide range of personal freedoms. The courts have described liberty as fundamental rights that are "essential to the orderly pursuit of happiness by free men." The due process clause declares that no STATE can deprive a citizen of the United States of a substantive right WITHOUT according that citizen due process of the law.

This clause has major implications for educators for several reasons. It makes the earlier amendments applicable to the states. Prior to the Fourteenth Amendment, the earlier amendments applied to the federal government only. Another important factor lies in the nature of public education; it is a state governmental function. When educators are acting in their professional capacities, they are “the state”. So, when administrators interact with teachers and students, they must be sure that they are functioning in a way that does not deprive an individual of his/her substantive rights.

In addition to the substantive interests cited above, the freedoms identified in the earlier amendments are considered substantive. For example, if a teacher is fired from his/her position for speaking out on an issue of public interest in the middle of the school year, the teacher could bring legal action in the federal courts because the state (the school system) deprived him/her of free speech rights. The teacher would also have to be accorded procedural due process because of the property interest in the remainder the annual contract. In another example, before a student can be suspended for a significant period of time, he/she must be accorded procedural due process because the right to an education accrues to the student as a property interest through the state constitution. The sources of substantive rights are multiple and varied, but regardless of the source, the due process clause of the Fourteenth Amendment will protect them. The major elements of procedural due process are notice, a hearing, and an impartial tribunal.

**Skill 4.14 Judicial and legislative provisions for students with disabilities, privacy act, affirmative action, sex discrimination, freedom of information, and civil rights**

ORELA 9.5

The **Individuals with Disabilities Education Act** (IDEA) was originally enacted by Congress in 1975 to make sure that, like other children, children with disabilities had the opportunity to receive a free appropriate public education. The most recent amendments were passed by Congress in December 2004, with final regulations published in August 2006. In some senses, the law is very new, even though it has a long, detailed, and powerful history. IDEA guides how states and school districts provide special education and related services to more than six million eligible children with disabilities.

The **Family Educational Rights and Privacy Act** (FERPA) (20 U.S.C. § 1232g; 34 CFR Part 99) is a Federal law that protects the privacy of student education records. The law applies to all schools that receive funds under an applicable program of the U.S. Department of Education. FERPA gives parents certain rights with respect to their children's education records. These rights transfer to the student when he or she reaches the age of 18 or attends a school beyond the high school level. Students to whom the rights have transferred are "eligible students."

**Title IX**, The Educational Amendments of 1972, states that no individual shall be excluded from participation in, be denied the benefits of, or be subjected to discrimination under any educational program or activity that receives or benefits from federal assistance on the basis of sex. This statute covers the areas of admission, educational programs and activities, access to course offerings, counseling and the use of appraisal and counseling materials, marital or parental status, and athletics. *Marshall v. Kirkland*

**Title VI, The Civil Rights Act** of 1964 extends protection from discrimination on the basis of race, color, or national origin in any program or activity receiving federal financial assistance. Title VII, The Civil Rights Act of 1964 states that it is unlawful for an employer to discriminate against any individual with respect to compensation, terms, conditions, or privileges of employment because of an individual's race, color, religion, sex, or national origin. Some exceptions are noted in this statute. It does not apply to religious organizations that seek individuals of a particular religion to perform the work of that organization. Where suspect classifications (those classifications having no basis in rationality) represent bona fide occupational qualifications, they are permitted. Classifications based upon merit and seniority are also acceptable under this statute. See *Ansonia BOE v. Philbrook.*

Skill 9.6 Demonstrating knowledge of how specific laws at the local, state, and federal level affect districts and residents

**PRAXIS Skill 4.7 Roles of various formal and informal organizations and agencies**

**PRAXIS Skill 4.6 Educational functions of local, state, and federal agencies and governing bodies**

**Skill 4.6 Educational functions of local, state, and federal agencies and governing bodies**

ORELA 9.6

In the United States, education is primarily a state and local responsibility. Business, churches, and communities can establish schools. However, regardless of who establishes a school, there are state standards that all schools must use in developing the curriculum for each subject and grade level. The federal government is able to make policy decisions and directives only for programs to which it provides funding (such programs include Title 1, Reading First, etc.). The state government is the primary legal decision-making authority and funder of public school districts. The structure of education finance in America reflects the predominant role of states and local governments. Of an estimated $909 billion being spent nationwide on education at all levels for school year 2004-2005, about 90 percent comes from state, local, and private sources.

In school districts, the board of directors or trustees determines the school district's budget and oversees the operation of the schools within the district. Schools receive the money from the state, but each school also has a budget which can be augmented through fundraising. Schools may have a parent council, which helps the school to keep operating. These councils provide parents with a voice in what takes place such as reviewing the school budget and approving fund-raising ventures.

The duties of local school boards include:

- Adopting rules and regulations governing teachers and students in all schools
- Determining the budget for each school
- Hiring teachers
- Establishing the standards for the curriculum and choosing the textbooks
- Serving as adjudicators in the dismissal of teachers and students

## Skill 4.7 Roles of various formal and informal organizations and agencies

ORELA 9.6

See previous Skill for information about roles of school boards

A school does not rely solely on the school board and the teachers for support. There are many outside agencies involved in the operation of a school. Local law enforcement agents may visit the school to make safety presentations to the students. They also want to make their presence known so students can seek their help if they need it. They take on the role of teachers in helping students to learn the proper ways to behave both inside and outside the school. This allows local officers to build relationships with students and the school community, this further benefits the community.

Health professionals, such as school nurses, speech pathologists, social workers and mental health practitioners, are also part of the school system. They come into the school on a regular basis or as they are needed to help both students and teachers.

Informally, parents and local businesses have a role to play within a school. Parents want to know what is happening in the school and this can be done through the parent council. However, parents are also visible in the school as volunteers helping teachers in the classroom or serving as chaperones for field trips and events. Businesses show their support for the school by providing funding for events or school projects. Extra resources are also provided outside the school such as with museums or in school such as with enrichment or extra-curricular opportunities for students such as athletics, fine arts, mentoring, tutoring, and community education programs for parents and families.

www.ingramcontent.com/pod-product-compliance
Lightning Source LLC
LaVergne TN
LVHW061247100826
845148LV00008B/1049

* 9 7 8 1 6 0 7 8 7 1 7 4 3 *